SMART KID, CAN'T READ

SMART KID, CAN'T READ

5 STEPS ANY PARENT CAN TAKE
TO GET HELP

LORNA KAUFMAN, PHD
WITH SANDRA DORAN, EDD, AND LEIGH LEVEEN

Published by Ash Point Publishing Group.
Boston, Massachusetts
info@smartkidcantread.com

www.SmartKidCantRead.com

ISBN: 978-0-9970789-1-6

Printed in the United States of America

Library of Congress Cataloguing-in-Publication Data is available upon request.

TABLE OF CONTENTS

STEP ONE
Act as Soon as You Suspect a Problem

STEP TWO
Understand What Your Child Needs

STEP THREE
Learn About the Reading Process

STEP FOUR
Know Your Legal Rights

STEP FIVE
Advocate for Your Child

ACKNOWLEDGMENTS

This book grew out of a passion—my lifelong commitment to helping children learn to read. The manuscript would still be sitting unfinished on my desk if it were not for the support, persistence, and love of Leigh Leveen and Sandra Doran. Sandy, a gifted writer and expert in curriculum development, helped to make this a readable book. I will always be grateful for her friendship, unfailing good humor, and consistent patience through endless versions. Leigh was my partner who shepherded the process through to publication. She tried to teach her mother about technology in the 21st century while at the same time raising two children and working. I am fortunate to have such a daughter.

My husband Gordon was a source of unending support and enthusiasm. His insights and suggestions have consistently raised the level of the book. I am grateful for his willingness to live with my preoccupation with the project. Special thanks are due to my son, David, who tended my gardens while I wrote.

And to the friends and colleagues who devoted precious time reading chapters and providing feedback. Nancy Mather has unparalleled expertise in developing testing materials, and her encouragement was important in developing the self-administered tests. Tom Mela and Beth Simon, two outstanding special educational attorneys, gave valuable insights into special education law. Miriam Stringer, a first-rate, experienced educational advocate, provided insight into parent advocacy. Mary Beth Fletcher and Susan Miller are two of the best reading therapists I have ever met. They know all there is to know about teaching struggling readers. They gave generously of their expertise and provided feedback on several chapters. Barbara Wilson knows what works and sharpened my understanding of what works. Her contributions to the manuscript were invaluable. Kira Armstrong, a first-rate neuropsychologist who understands reading, helped shape the evaluation chapter.

I am especially indebted to Peggy McCardle, who was central to the writing of this book. She greatly strengthened the content while editing the manuscript. Her expertise and support helped guide the project to completion.

My heartfelt gratitude to Michelle Farley and Patricia Papernow, two parents who became dear friends and were involved in the writing of this book. I can't thank them enough for their willingness to challenge me to say what needed to be said from a parent's perspective. Many other friends and colleagues have provided insights and support during this project; Liz Glover, Stuart Horwitz, Dale Slongwhite, and Amin Ahmad provided support, feedback, and assistance.

This book began with parent focus groups. The ideas generated in those discussions form the basis of what you find in these pages. Many thanks to those who gave of their time to participate: Carol Otto, Gail Sheehan, Kristin Boardman, Ellie Hickey, and Lorraine Devin.

And finally, heartfelt thanks to the many parents of children I have evaluated and worked with over 30 years of practice. I am both humbled by and impressed with their steely perseverance as they pursued what was best for their children. I have seen parents take out second mortgages on their homes, move to different communities, and give up their savings to secure the education their children needed. While wisdom can't be told, these parents were a wellspring of knowledge, insights, and inspiration. They strengthened my faith in reasoned advocacy as an important tool for improving children's reading skills.

—Lorna Nickerson Kaufman
August 2015

OUR NATIONAL SHAME

"For a country like America to be leaving behind about 38 to 40 percent of its youngsters in terms of not learning to read is unconscionable!"[1]

—Reid Lyon, PhD
Former Chief of Child Development and Behavior Branch
National Institute of Child Health and Human Development
National Institutes of Health

We are failing our children when we are unable to provide them with the reading skills they require to lead productive and fulfilling lives.

While you may not be aware of it, there are children and adults in your life who are challenged to read the simplest material we all take for granted: newspapers, forms, labels, and directions. Their struggle to read impacts their lives at every level. This serious reading crisis affects our economy and our democracy, and contributes to every major social concern in the country. But reading failure also affects our children in deeply personal ways. Children with reading problems often feel a deep sense of shame. They try to cover it up in a number of ways. As a developmental psychologist with over 30 years of experience working with students of

---

1   "Dr. G. Reid Lyon: Converging Evidence—Reading Research—What It Takes to Read," by Children of the Code, 2014. Retrieved from http://www.childrenofthecode.org/interviews/lyon.htm.

all ages, I have observed the disastrous effects reading problems have on our children. And I have also rejoiced with families who have beat the odds and found a way to help their children meet with success.

What happens when children find themselves in a pattern of reading failure with no one to advocate for them? Some, like Jerry, act out and develop behavioral problems. Jerry was an energetic and personable fourth grader whose teachers complained that he distracted the class and often played the class clown. They believed that Jerry's real problem was his inability to pay attention.

Other children, like Beth, an anxious and unhappy sixth grader, may withdraw and hope no one will realize the extent of their difficulty. Beth was quiet in class and never volunteered to read out loud. Her teachers thought she was doing well and were not aware of her struggle with reading. However, Beth had serious "meltdowns" at home when it came time to complete her homework. She could not read any of her assignments independently, and her mother spent hours trying to help her every night.

Some, like Jefferson, a handsome, independently minded teenager, believe they will never learn to read, and eventually give up. By the time Jefferson entered high school, he had decided to drop out of school as soon as he could. His feelings of failure and shame not only impeded his ability to learn but also became part of his problem. These feelings would impact the course of his life.

Reading is not simply an academic skill. In today's world, reading difficulty has repercussions far beyond schoolwork.

It is clear that children who do not develop proficient literacy skills will have trouble functioning as adults in our society. They will have difficulty in the workplace and problems participating in the mainstream culture. Low literacy skills have a high personal cost. Individuals who struggle to read suffer from a sense of shame and depression, and a loss of self-esteem. Even the brightest children, when suffering from unaddressed reading difficulties, are seldom able to achieve their personal potential.

Some schools would like to mask this sober reality. I often hear teachers tell parents that children who struggle with reading no longer need to endure the "tedious process" of remediation. "Technology will take care of reading problems," they say. With the advent of spell checkers and text-to-speech and speech-to-text programs, technology is indeed capable of addressing many problems. However, it is not the answer for children who lack basic reading and writing skills. Even the savviest use of technology is no substitute for effective literacy skills.

THE LINK BETWEEN READING PROBLEMS AND SOCIETAL PROBLEMS

"Every social pathology appears to be related to literacy attainment."[2]

—Dr. Timothy Shanahan
Professor and Director
University of Illinois at Chicago Center for Literacy

The statistical links between reading problems and societal problems are well documented:

- 88% of high school dropouts struggle with reading.[3]

- 70% of prison inmates read below a fourth grade level.

- 85% of all juveniles who interface with the juvenile court system are functionally illiterate. The Department of Justice states, "the link between academic failure and delinquency, violence, and crime is welded to reading failure."[4]

---

2 "Dr. Timothy Shanahan—The Personal and Social Implications of Literacy and Literacy Instruction," by Children of the Code, 2014. Retrieved from *www.childrenofthecode.org/interviews/shanahan.htm.*
3 *Early Warning! Why Reading at the End of the Third Grade Matters,* by Annie E. Casey Foundation, 2010. Retrieved from http://www.aecf.org/m/resourcedoc/AECF-Early_Warning_Full_Report-2010.pdf.
4 "Literacy Statistics," by Begin to Read, n.d. Retrieved from http://www.begintoread.com/research/literacystatistics.html.

The relationship between literacy and poverty is clear:[5]

▶ Approximately three out of four people on welfare can't read.

▶ 46%–51% of American adults have an income well below the poverty level because of their inability to read.

WHAT DOES LITERACY MEAN FOR AN ADULT?

Individuals who have difficulty reading do not all have the same skill levels. Reading problems can best be viewed as existing on a continuum of severity. In 2003 the National Assessment of Adult Literacy classified individuals over 16 by their ability to read and understand basic health information and services needed to make appropriate health decisions. They classified adults into the following categories:

▶ *Proficient literacy skills* (13% of the adult population): Can read lengthy, complex, abstract text to synthesize information and draw abstract inferences.

▶ *Intermediate literacy skills* (53% of the population): Can read and understand moderately dense commonplace text; able to summarize and make moderate inferences.

▶ *Basic literacy skills* (29% of the population): Can read and understand information in short commonplace prose.

▶ *Below basic literacy skills* (14% of the population): Possess skills that range from being nonliterate in English to having the ability to locate easily identifiable information in short, commonplace text.[6]

5   "Staggering Illiteracy Statistics," by Literacy Project Foundation, n.d. Retrieved from literacyprojectfounda-tion.org/community/statistics.
6   "National Assessment of Adult Literacy (NAAL): Demographics—Overall," by National Center for Education Statistics, n.d. Retrieved from nces.ed.gov/naal/kf_demographics.asp.

ILLITERACY IN THE UNITED STATES

Adults in our society who have difficulty reading and writing often have trouble with employment and supporting their families. Forty-five million adults in our society read below a fifth-grade level. Many of these adults are also parents. They cannot read simple stories to their own children. They do not possess the skills to support and promote literacy[7] in their children and are not able to provide them with the rich early language and literacy experiences that we know to be so important to their reading development. *The profound sense of personal shame that these children and adults endure is our national shame.*

WE'VE KNOWN ABOUT THIS PROBLEM FOR MANY YEARS

The National Institute of Child Health and Human Development (NICHD), a division of the National Institutes of Health (NIH), has been funding research on the issue of reading for more than three decades. The results of this research tell us who is having trouble learning to read, why they are having trouble, and what can be done about it. We have learned how good readers learn to read and how this process differs in children who struggle to learn to read. We have learned how best to teach reading and how to help struggling readers.

In 2000, NICHD published a major report, *Teaching Children to Read: The Report of the National Reading Panel.*[8] This report provides us with a clear picture of what we must do to improve reading instruction in our schools and reduce the number of children who struggle with literacy. It is stunning how few educators and parents are aware of this important research. Most devastating for our children, very few

---

7   "Literacy" is a term that is used in many different ways. Recently the field has defined it to include both reading and writing. However, in this book, I will generally use it to refer to reading issues.

8   "National Reading Panel," by National Institute of Child Health and Human Development, 2013. Retrieved from http://www.nichd.nih.gov/research/supported/Pages/nrp.aspx.

of the clear, research-based recommendations in the report have been put into place.

ARE READING PROBLEMS COMMON?

Reading problems exist in every public school in the country and affect children from all socioeconomic backgrounds. However, African American, American Indian, and Hispanic children have the highest rates of reading difficulty. The most recent assessment, completed in 2009 by the National Assessment of Educational Progress (NAEP), reported that among fourth graders:[9]

▸ 53% of African American children read at or below a "basic" level

▸ 52% of Hispanic children read at or below a "basic" level

▸ 48% of American Indian children read at or below a "basic" level

In a landmark study in 1998, the NAEP reported that 38% of all children entering the fourth grade were reading below a basic skill level. A follow-up study in 2013 indicated only a slight improvement. They reported that 32% of students were below a basic level in reading, 33% were at a basic level, and 35% were proficient or above.[10] In other words, *only about one third of our readers are good, proficient readers.* A student needs to read at a proficient level to be able to learn effectively from what he reads.

This means a high percentage of fourth graders are seriously below grade expectations in their ability to read. Most of these children will continue to struggle with reading throughout their school

---

9   "Literacy Facts and Stats," by Reading Is Fundamental, n.d. Retrieved from www.rif.org/us/about/litera-cy-facts-and-stats.htm.
10   "A First Look: 2013 Mathematics and Reading," by National Center for Education Statistics, n.d., p. 7. Retrieved from http://nces.ed.gov/nationsreportcard/subject/publications/main2013/pdf/2014451.pdf.

careers and will never catch up with their peers. Many of them will drop out of school.

Even more troubling, the NAEP found that less than one third of the children who were reading below grade-level actually received reading

> **FACT:** You need to read at the proficient level to really learn from reading.

help. *The help that is given to many students who struggle with reading is often not adequate or appropriate.*

Millions of children in our country receive special education services in school, costing our school systems billions of dollars. Nearly two thirds of all children who receive special education services are children with reading problems. "Reading problems are the overwhelming reason that children are identified as having learning disabilities and receive special education services."[11] We are spending billions of dollars on a problem that we know how to prevent.

> **FACT:** Most reading problems can be prevented. We are spending billions of dollars on a problem that we know how to prevent.

The data is clear. We know the extent of our literacy issues, and we know how to address them. The fact that we continue to leave one third of our students behind

with low literacy skills is a national shame and a disservice to our children. Despite all we know, many schools have not been able to address this problem. That leaves it up to you to take the lead for your child.

HOW TO USE THIS BOOK

This book is written for all those who are in a position to advocate for and help children who struggle to read: parents, grandparents,

---

11　*The Voice of Evidence in Reading Research* (p. xxvii), by P. McCardle and V. Chhabra, 2004, Baltimore, MD: Paul H. Brooks.

guardians, and teachers in particular. It contains practical advice based on my work with parents and school systems for more than 30 years. The cases you will read are based on actual families that I have known in my practice. While names and some facts are changed to protect identities, these are real children. (Also, because both boys and girls may struggle with learning to read, I will vary between using the personal pronouns "he" and "she," and will use the relevant pronoun for the child in the example at the beginning of each chapter.)

Over the years parents have urged me to write this book. When I finally decided to take on the task, I put together parent focus groups to hear what mothers and fathers felt were the most crucial points for helping other families just beginning their journey. The themes that came out of those discussions, along with my professional experience, form the basis of what you will find in these pages. There is some theoretical information where needed, but mostly you will find "advice from the trenches."

The book outlines five steps aimed at empowering parents to take an active role in their child's education. *Children whose parents advocate on their behalf receive more reading help, and better quality reading help, than children whose parents are not involved.*

Step One: *Act as Soon as You Suspect a Problem*

Step one is critical. You must act as soon as you suspect that your child is having difficulty reading. Children do not just "outgrow" reading problems. Once children enter the fourth grade, it is much more difficult to help them catch up with their peers. The first chapter explains why parents should act as soon as they suspect a problem. You will learn why schools tend to "kick the can down the road," and why parents are often reluctant to take action.

Parents are sometimes confused about whether their child is reading at grade level and don't know when they should act. The teacher advises them not to worry, but parents see their child struggling. For those parents who face this dilemma, Chapter 2 provides information about the reading skills that children should have by the end of each grade as they are first learning to read. A series of informal screening tests that parents can administer to their own children is found in Appendices A–E. These informal tests are easy to administer to children and will give you a general idea of whether your concerns are justified.

Step Two: *Understand What Your Child Needs*

You must have a full and accurate understanding of your child's academic needs. Information that is unbiased and free from the budgetary and personnel concerns of the school system is essential to developing an effective game plan for getting help with reading. This information about your child's needs is the backbone of your advocacy plan. Chapter 3 explains why this information must come from an unbiased, independent evaluation completed by a skilled professional outside the school system. As part of the second step, you will learn in Chapter 4 how to understand those test results.

Step Three: *Learn About the Reading Process*

You need to learn enough about the reading process to effectively advocate for the specific, evidence-based reading instruction your child needs. You must be able to determine whether your child is receiving reading instruction that will result in his becoming a successful reader. In Chapter 5 you will learn how children acquire reading skills and why some children struggle to learn. In Chapter 6 you will learn how to tell the difference between an effective reading program and an ineffective program. You will learn what works for both beginning readers and for struggling readers.

Step Four: *Know Your Legal Rights*

To be effective, you need to know what the law says about your rights. The federal special education law (IDEA 2004) provides you and your child with legal safeguards and outlines the procedures schools must follow when providing children with special education services. Chapter 7 provides a primer on the special education law. You will learn the importance of knowing how to use your legal rights when advocating for services for your child.

Step Five: *Advocate for Your Child*

You must learn to advocate for your child. Once you understand what your child needs and you know the critical elements of an effective reading program, you can use the information to advocate for your child. Armed with knowledge about your legal rights and a determination to see that your child learns to read, you will be able to move ahead. This step provides practical advice on how to advocate effectively for better reading services with your school system.

There is a lot of information in these chapters. Take a look at the table of contents so that you know what is here for you. You may choose to read the whole book straight through, or you may want to

STEP ONE

Act as Soon as
You Suspect a Problem

CHAPTER ONE

DON'T WAIT—THE NEED TO ACT EARLY

"Parents need to be aware that if a child is in trouble, they must seek help immediately. The longer the child practices reading and spelling using the wrong strategy, the further he will fall behind his classmates. All the evidence shows conclusively that poor readers do not catch up simply because they get older. Don't believe any teacher who tells you this."[12]

—Diane McGuinness, PhD
Author, *Why Our Children Can't Read,*
and What We Can Do About It

The most important piece of advice I can give to parents who suspect their child has a reading problem comes from the mother of a young boy with dyslexia: *Seek help as soon as you suspect a problem . . . and don't quit until you find a solution.*

In my practice as a specialist on reading disabilities, I have observed many different outcomes through the years as I have watched parents react to their children's struggles to read. Two cases illustrate the need for early identification: 6-year-old Amy and 13-year-old Jamal.

---

12   *Why Our Children Can't Read, and What We Can Do About It* (p. 328), by D. McGuinness, 1999, New York, NY: Touchstone.

Amy literally danced into my office. A tall first-grader, she whirled and twirled as she showed me the ballet steps she had just learned. Her dancing and constant chatter seemed to mask her anxiety about being in a new place. I tried to begin my evaluation, but then my cat wandered into the office, and Amy was distracted once again, playing with the cat and not listening to my questions. Finally, we managed to settle down, and her story emerged.

Amy's grandmother had sent the little girl to me. Despite her clear intelligence and ability to do math, Amy found it hard to read at the first-grade level. She could write her own name and identify all the letters of the alphabet, but the sounds of letters often escaped her. Amy managed to get along by identifying the first sounds of a few words and using the pictures in her storybooks to guess the rest. Her teachers had decided she had **attention-deficit/hyperactivity disorder (ADHD)** *and needed medication. Despite their assurances that she was young and her reading would improve in time, her grandmother saw it differently.*

Attention-deficit/ hyperactivity disorder (ADHD): A persistent pattern of inattention and/or hyperactivity-impulsivity that interferes with functioning or development. Several symptoms need to be present in more than one setting to qualify for a diagnosis. It is not a learning disability, although some children may have ADHD as well as a reading disability.

My evaluation confirmed Amy's grandmother's insight. Amy had a reading disability. In fact, she was having a very difficult time blending sounds together to form words. Her school still maintained that she was not "that far behind" and was too young to receive extra help in reading. Her parents armed themselves with my evaluation and began a long struggle with the school system. Finally, they reached a workable solution. The school would provide Amy with small-group specialized reading help, and her parents would pay for private, one-on-one, after-school tutoring. The school agreed to coordinate their reading program with that of the tutor's by having the reading teacher speak with the tutor every 2 weeks. After a year and a half of this effort, Amy blossomed into a successful reader, and was reading above her grade level by the end of the third grade.

Amy's story had a happy ending because her parents were willing to advocate for her. I have met other children for whom the outcome was not as positive.

When Jamal walked into my office, he was silent and with-drawn. Over 6 feet tall in the ninth grade, this handsome high school freshman already faced limited options for the rest of his life. Jamal's school had decided that the best thing for him was to engage in "work-study." He was to be apprenticed to a business in the suburb where he lived, returning to high school only for vocational classes.

When I tested him, Jamal was reading at a second-grade level. I told his concerned mother that he would need specialized reading instruction on a daily basis in order to improve. I also told her that, given the severity of his disability and his signif-icant delays in reading, he would require a specialized school where he could receive instruction appropriate to his needs.

But Jamal's mother was reluctant to confront the public school. A single parent, she had bootstrapped herself out of poverty and obtained her teaching degree. She had recently started teaching within the very school system I was telling her to confront. Understandably, Jamal's mother was reluctant to act. She was worried about losing her job and about repercussions for her son. She did not confront the school or demand the specialized reading instruction that Jamal so desperately needed. Jamal continued with this "work-study" program and graduated from high school with no basic literacy skills, thus forcing him into the unskilled labor force and leaving him at emotional risk.

Amy and Jamal represent two examples of extreme cases. Amy was identified at a young age by her grandmother, who recognized she was having trouble learning to read. Her parents were unwilling to accept the school's response that she would learn in "her own time" and insisted on getting her help with reading in the first grade. As a result, Amy became a fluent and avid reader by the time she completed the third grade. In contrast, Jamal's mother did not act on her earlier suspicions that the reading help he was receiving in school was not working. She waited until he was in the ninth grade before getting an independent, diagnostic evaluation, and then was unable to act on the recommendations. Jamal was condemned to spend the rest of his life unable to read well, with severely limited job options.

It's very common for parents to be concerned about repercussions for their children and for themselves when they challenge the school system. However, it is entirely possible to disagree with the school without fear that your disagreement will be taken out on your child.

In my experience, if you treat teachers and administrators with respect and come armed with good information, there is seldom cause to fear repercussions. It is particularly valuable to bring an outside expert when you attend meetings to challenge the school and to advocate for your child. This further reduces the chances of repercussions. Many parents

> **TIP:** It is possible to disagree with your school system without fear that your disagreement will result in repercussions on your child.

find that teachers will privately agree with them but are unable to speak up in a meeting because of pressure from their supervisors.

TRUST YOUR INSTINCTS AS A PARENT

Parents are often the first to notice reading problems. As a parent, you are your child's first—and most important—teacher and role model. You taught your child self-regulatory behaviors, such as sleeping, eating, impulse control, and toilet training. You are the role model for language development. You taught your child words, songs, and stories. You have read books to him for years and know whether he can sit still and listen to a story. You have observed your child's language development and know how it compares to that of other children of the same age. You know how he responds to situations

> **ACT:** If you think your child is having trouble learning to read, trust your instincts and check it out.

and how he behaves when he is stressed. You have a lot of information about your child's development and how he learns. If you think your child is having trouble learning to read, *trust your instincts.*

It is not easy to face the fact that your child is not making the progress he should be making. It is so comforting to listen to the people who tell you that everything will be fine, that he just needs more time. It requires conviction and a well-informed parent to disagree with teachers, well-meaning grandparents, or even principals, and act against their advice.

In the pages of this book, you will acquire the courage and knowledge you need to advocate for your child.

REASONS SCHOOLS DON'T ACT AS SOON AS THEY SEE A PROBLEM

There are many reasons that reading problems among young children are not identified early, in kindergarten, first, or even second grade.

▶ **A classroom teacher must divide her attention** among many children. No teacher is as focused on your child as you are. There may be other children in the same classroom who are even further behind. The teacher may not see your child as having significant problems relative to others with more serious concerns.

▶ **The teacher may have lower expectations for your child than you have.** The teacher may assume that your child is just a *slow learner* and will eventually learn to read.

▶ **Many teachers are not well informed about reading problems** and do not understand the importance of early identification. They are often unaware of the consequences of waiting. They are not focused on the *cumulative effect* of 4 to 5 years of falling further behind in reading. They are focused only on what happens in their classroom during that year of your child's schooling.

▶ **A teacher's goal is usually to follow the curriculum.** Students in the middle are the primary focus. High and low achievers require extra effort.

▶ **The teacher may assume that the problem is "just developmental"** and your child will learn in time. Parents frequently hear teachers say, "He will learn when he is ready." Often schools hope the problem will go away or that the student will start to learn at a later time. Perhaps the child will "outgrow" the problem.

▶ **It can be costly for the school to identify a child** as having a reading problem. In most school systems this recognition will trigger an evaluation and reading help. These are both costly actions for schools. For this very reason, teachers in many school districts are discouraged from referring children at too young an age.

Countless teachers have told me stories of how they have been advised by administrators not to recommend services for a particular child. It is very common for teachers to privately tell parents that their child needs help but they cannot speak up publicly in a meeting or make the recommendation. Schools will never admit that there is a financial reason for not identifying children, but cost is always a factor.

These points can be painful to accept. Just when you need your school system to provide you with expert advice, you realize it has

> **FACT:** School districts have many reasons for not identifying reading problems early.

many conflicting agendas. I will never forget the words of one mother who struggled with this issue.

"It took me a long time to understand this fact. The more I learned, the more I realized the teachers did not understand the severity of my child's problem. It also seemed the higher

the grade, the less they knew about reading. I remember Sam's fourth grade orientation night: Parents were sitting at the desks and I heard, 'We are no longer learning to read—we are reading to learn.' My heart sank to the floor below. We were in trouble. Even Einstein would have been trouble in this classroom."

REASONS PARENTS DON'T ACT AS SOON AS THEY SUSPECT A PROBLEM

▶ **As parents, we want to avoid labeling our children.** We all want our children to grow up free of problems. It is a perfectly normal response to want to protect our children from being labeled as having "special needs."

Some parents fear that the stigma of "labeling" will make their son or daughter feel different. It is important to understand that students who have trouble reading *already* feel different. Frequently the student feels completely alone and is the only person admitting the existence of the problem. Children do not understand that struggling with reading doesn't mean they aren't smart. They see other children who do not seem to be struggling at all. It is easy to conclude, "I'm stupid." Children can become discouraged and begin to feel hopeless. I have never met a first, second, or third grade student who did not welcome the opportunity to get the help he needed—provided the help made a difference and resulted in improvement.

▶ **As parents, we may not understand there is an underlying problem.** Struggling readers may sometimes try to hide the fact they can't read, or they may act out. For example, some children develop a keen sense of humor or become the class clown. Others become very anxious. Many children show spurts of anger or hostility to those close to them. Some children withdraw and avoid interaction.

But, deep inside, these children know they have a problem. It frequently comes as a great relief to children when the adults in their lives acknowledge and identify the trouble they are having. This identification is not a stigma if it brings with it the appropriate help. *Your child is depending on you to help him. He can't act on his own behalf.*

> **ACT:** Your child is depending on you to help him. He can't act on his own behalf.

▶ **As parents we may not understand the implications of falling behind classmates in reading skills.** Few parents understand the seriousness of falling below grade-level in reading at an early age. Many assume their children will catch up and everything will be fine. In reality, if your child is not at grade level by the end of third grade, it is extremely difficult for him to catch up with his peers unless he has intensive remediation.

You need to believe in your child when everyone else gives up on him. It is important not to blame a child or make him feel that there is something wrong with him. Avoid using words like "lazy." Some adults become impatient when students exhibit difficulty with reading and tell them to "try harder" or "pay more attention." If they could, they would. Children who are struggling with reading will not improve when yelled at or criticized. Improvement comes from specialized, appropriate instruction with a teacher who is qualified to work with struggling readers and from compassionate and empathetic parents. As parents, we may not understand the seriousness of an unresolved reading problem.

If your child had any kind of a medical problem, you would seek help right away. If, for example, he began to feel tired, experience muscle weakness, lose his appetite, and experience pain, would you ignore it and hope he would "outgrow it?" Of course not. These symptoms could be signs of a serious medical problem, but one that might be easily treated if caught early. If you decided to wait for a year, the problem might become more serious and your child might develop complications. Treatment would be more difficult and take longer. Now imagine waiting for 3 years! Reading problems need to be managed with the same level of attention and care. An unresolved reading problem can become life changing.

> **WARNING:** An unresolved reading problem can become life changing.

FIVE REASONS FOR ACTING AS SOON AS YOU SUSPECT A PROBLEM

1. **It is easier to help students before they get too far behind their classmates.**

    We know from years of reading research that more than 90% of students who are behind in reading by the beginning of the fourth grade will never catch up with their classmates. Most will remain behind in reading for the rest of their school years and will not achieve their full intellectual potential without serious and very intensive intervention efforts.

    Does this mean that children are doomed if they are behind in the fourth grade? No! It means that if they enter the fourth grade (or a later grade) behind their peers in reading, catching up requires a huge amount of time and effort. Few school systems and few students are able to invest the amount of time, money, and effort needed to accelerate learning and bring students up to grade level once they are so far behind.

Additionally, younger students are not usually resistant to help because they do not yet see it as socially unacceptable. Older students are often more worried about peer acceptance. They often go to great lengths to try to hide their reading disability from their friends and classmates. They may get caught in a cycle of shame and embarrassment because they cannot read as well as their classmates.

2. Reading is fundamental to all learning that takes place in school.

In the early grades (kindergarten, first, second, and third grades) a significant portion of each school day is devoted to teaching children to read. By the fourth grade, students are expected to read fluently and to use their reading skills to acquire new information in science, social studies, language arts, and math. The fundamental skills in reading are no longer stressed after third grade.

FACT: Most children who are below grade level in reading at the beginning of fourth grade will not be able to catch up with their peers.

A student who cannot read at grade level will have trouble keeping up in all subjects. Science, social studies, language arts, and even math require the student to read and write well. Children who cannot read their grade-level textbooks will not be able to keep pace with their peers.

3. Children with reading problems often hold themselves in low esteem, putting themselves at risk for a host of other problems.

Children who have trouble acquiring basic reading skills are at risk of viewing themselves as failures. After all, they have not been successful at mastering the basic skills so strongly stressed by their teachers and valued by their parents. Some will "act out," while others try to hide their reading problems, developing elaborate compensatory strategies to cover up their inability to read.

For example, children with good verbal reasoning ability can often successfully guess at words by looking at pictures and understanding the general story content. Many children get by with this strategy until the reading content becomes too difficult to be able to accurately predict words. *Guessing is never a substitute for reading.* I am

> **FACT:** Guessing is never a substitute for reading.

always surprised at the number of educators who seem unaware that these compensatory strategies often disguise weak reading skills. Many students give up, believing they will never learn.

4. **There are evidence-based methods for remedying reading problems in the early grades.**

   We know how to help children who are having difficulty acquiring reading skills. These methods have been available for more than 50 years from teachers in well-informed school systems, specialized tutors, and private schools that specialize in working with dyslexic students. They are now offered in more and more public schools throughout the country.

5. **Start early—the process for getting reading help for your child may take longer than you expect.**

There are federal and state laws regulating the time frames for completing an evaluation and providing help for a student. However, the reality is that it can frequently

> **TIP:** Start early—the process for getting reading help may take longer than you expect.

take the better part of a school year from the time you ask for help to the time your child begins to receive help.

ACT NOW

Do not wait for the problem to get worse. You cannot assume that your child will outgrow his struggle with reading. Reading problems do not just disappear. Monitor your child's reading progress by asking him to read pages from his books out loud. In kindergarten, first, second, and third grade, when he is first learning to read, make certain that he is learning to read accurately, fluently, and with good comprehension. As he gets older, continue to have him read orally on a periodic basis to make certain that he is able

> **TIP:** Reading problems can be fixed, but it is not possible to fix a problem until it is first acknowledged.

to manage the reading as it increases in length and difficulty. The following informal monitoring can be a first step:

- ▶ Ask your child to read the papers and books he brings home from school. Can he read his classroom books and papers *accurately, fluently, and with comprehension?*

- ▶ Get some grade-appropriate books from your library and see if your child is able to read them. Most librarians can be very helpful in guiding you to such books.

▶ Meet with the classroom teacher to ask questions about your child's reading progress. If you see that he is having trouble by the end of the first grade, it is time to act.

If you continue to have questions about your child's reading ability, check out the grade-level guidelines in the next chapter and administer one of the informal screening tests found in the appendix.

CHAPTER TWO

HOW DO I KNOW IF MY CHILD HAS A READING PROBLEM?

"In order to ensure that your child's reading development is on track, you need to know how to tell if your child is falling behind in reading, and you need to be able to recognize effective reading instruction."

—Susan L. Hall and Louisa C. Moats, EdD
Authors, *Parenting a Struggling Reader: A Guide to Diagnosing and Finding Help for Your Child's Reading Difficulties*[13]

I heard Suzanne's confusion when I first spoke with her on the phone. She had been referred by a friend who persuaded her that she must speak to someone outside the school system to get an objective, professional look at her son's reading ability. Suzanne explained that Jacob, her 8-year-old son, struggled to read the books and handouts he brought home from school. He could not complete his homework by himself because he had trouble reading. He was becoming frustrated. Jacob was developing stomachaches on school mornings and often found himself in the nurse's office. In fact, Suzanne had taken him

---

13   *Parenting a Struggling Reader: A Guide to Diagnosing and Finding Help for Your Child's Reading Difficulties* (p. 21), by S. Hall and L. Moats, 2002, New York, NY: Broadway Books.

to the pediatrician twice to check this out. Yet, his second grade
teacher said that he was doing fine. She assured Suzanne that
Jacob would catch on in time.
His difficulties were normal. She
said that boys were often less
mature than girls and some-

> **FACT:** Both boys and girls should be able to master reading skills in the first and second grades.

times took longer to learn to read. She said he was not at the
bottom of the class. Several other students were experiencing
the same thing.

Suzanne was confused and worried. She saw her son
struggling, but the teacher told her his issues were normal and
he would be fine. She saw her son guessing at words based on
pictures and their first letters. She realized that he did not know
how to sound out words. Was this really normal?

I explained to Suzanne that a student in the middle of the
second grade should have basic reading skills. He should be
able to read his homework and work papers from school. The
only way to know whether Jacob had those skills was to evaluate
him to determine his actual reading level. If he did not have
grade-appropriate skills, it would be important to determine
why he was having trouble and provide effective intervention
that would help him learn to read.

RED FLAGS FOR READING PROBLEMS

There are *behavioral, developmental,* and *educational* red flags that
can alert you to the possibility that your child may be having trouble
with reading. The signs are usually there; it is a matter of learning how
to interpret them. Suzanne had correctly identified several red flags.

Behavioral indicators. Many parents are sensitive to behaviors that signal problems at school but do not necessarily associate them with a reading problem. Children who start school enthusiastically may become reluctant to go to school and complain, "School is too boring." Like Jacob, they may develop stomachaches or headaches on school mornings and it may be hard to get them out of the house. They may resist reading out loud for you at home, and when they do, their reading is slow and laborious.

Some children become disruptive in school. Teachers report they are class clowns, disrupt other students, or are inattentive. Teachers often believe that a child is having trouble because of attention problems. Jacob had become very anxious about learning to read. This anxiety was making him fidgety, and he was in constant motion. He tried to avoid school.

> A **diagnostic evaluation** is a comprehensive assessment of a child given by a professional certified in the field of education or psychology.

He had stomachaches on school mornings. It is often difficult to determine which comes first: Is a child inattentive in class because he is having trouble learning, or is he having trouble learning because he is inattentive? A **diagnostic evaluation** is usually necessary to sort out this issue.

It is common for children to keep themselves together during school and appear to their teachers as if they are coping and learning well. Those same children may fall apart at home when it comes time to complete their work assignments. As they get older, they have trouble managing their homework independently because they are unable to read, write, or complete assignments without help.

I have listened to countless parents describe evenings with homework as a nightmare. Tantrums and significant meltdowns disrupt the whole family. Homework often takes hours to complete, much longer than it should. Students try to avoid doing assignments when they can't do the work independently. *When homework expectations are reasonable and within a child's ability level, nightly battles are not normal behavior.* Young children are naturally curious and want to learn. They enjoy developing adult-like skills and take pleasure in their accomplishments. If your first or second grader is not experiencing this joy in learning, check it out!

The 10-minute rule, formulated by the National Parent Teacher Association (NPTA),[14] is a reasonable guideline used by many parents and schools. The NPTA recommends that a child in the first grade should spend approximately 10–20 minutes per night on homework, and that homework should be increased by approximately 10 minutes per grade. Thus, a child in the second grade should spend approximately 20–30 minutes per night on homework, and a child in the fifth grade

---

THE NATIONAL PARENT TEACHER ASSOCIATION HOMEWORK RECOMMENDATIONS:

▶ First Grade: 10–20 minutes

▶ Second Grade: 20–30 minutes

▶ Third Grade: 30–40 minutes

▶ Fourth Grade: 40-50 minutes

▶ Fifth Grade: 50-60 minutes

Add 10 minutes for each succeeding grade.

---

14 "Research Spotlight on Homework," by National Education Association, n.d. Retrieved from www.nea.org/tools/16938.htm.

approximately 50–60 minutes per night. While there are normal variations in homework assignments, this is a good rule of thumb that can help you judge the approximate amount of time your child should spend on homework.

Developmental indicators. Reading is a skill that is related to a child's oral language development. As you watch your child learn to speak and understand language, be aware of red flags that may signal a risk for reading problems.

In the following list, it is important to note that the presence of even one of these markers can be significant. Your child does not need to have all of the markers in order to be at risk for a potential reading problem.

1. **Children who are slow in learning to speak are at risk for reading problems.** Though not all children who experience slow language development will develop reading problems, many will. The majority of children who come through our office for reading evaluations have a history of delayed oral language development. Many continue to exhibit either mild or, occasionally, severe problems in using language to express themselves as they get older. Some children cannot pronounce words correctly and may, for example, say "spaspetty" for spaghetti or "aminal" for animal long after this is developmentally appropriate.

    A young boy I saw recently provides a classic example of delayed language skills.

    Timmy's motor skills, such as crawling, walking, and climbing stairs developed well ahead of the normal time frames. His parents had high expectations. However, his language was slow in emerging. His grandparents still could not understand him on the phone by the time he was 4 years old. Timmy eventually learned to speak clearly, but he continued to have subtle difficulty expressing himself and organizing what he wanted to say in a clear way. His slow language development and continued difficulty expressing and organizing his ideas were symptomatic of an underlying problem with language. His use of syntax, vocabulary, and grammar continued to lag behind age expectations. As he grew older, these differences became less noticeable but interfered with his development of reading and written language skills. The same underlying language problems he had as a toddler contributed to the trouble he had learning to read and write.

2. **Some children may have difficulty attending to specific sounds in words.** You may notice, for example, when reading to your 3–5-year-old, that he is insensitive to rhymes. The ability to perceive rhyming and, when older, to produce rhymes is an important marker of a child's development of sensitivity to sounds in words.

> **FACT:** Reading is a skill that is related to a child's oral language development.

3. **Some children have difficulty organizing what they want to say.** A child may have good ideas but find it difficult to express them. For example, when 5-year-old Abby tried to describe her new dollhouse to her grandfather, she had difficulty organizing and sequencing her thoughts.

    Abby: "There is a bed upstairs and the chimney fell off and a pretty pink chair."

    Grandfather: "Was the chair in the bedroom?"

Abby: "No, downstairs. Then the dog ate my hotdog."

Grandfather: "You have a dog in your dollhouse?"

Abby: "No, silly. Bowser. My REAL dog."

While family members may understand what Abby is trying to say, most strangers would have difficulty understanding the flow of her ideas. As these children get older, their language may become more coherent, but if you listen carefully, you may detect continued difficulty in organizing and formulating ideas. You may also note organizational difficulties in their written language.

You can check out your child's ability to organize and formulate language by reading him a short story. Ask him to retell the story

> **ACT:** Check out your child's ability to organize and formulate language.

in his own words. Is he able to clearly remember and retell the story? Is he able to sequence the events correctly? Did he get the main point of the story?

4. **Some children have trouble finding the right words and use word fillers, such as "stuff" and "that thing," excessively.** Their language lacks specificity because they cannot find the right word, even though they may know it. They may have difficulty recalling proper names and titles. They frequently attempt to describe things rather than name them. A child might say, "The room where I sleep," rather than "my bedroom."

5. **Chronic ear infections appear to have an effect on language development and, later, on reading.** Many children with chronic ear infections experience intermittent hearing loss during early

childhood. This can impact their ability to hear the sounds of language at critical periods of development.

6. **Children with a family history of reading problems are also more likely to have trouble learning to read than children whose relatives did not have such problems.** If a child's parents, aunts, uncles, grandparents, or cousins had trouble learning to read, it is more likely that he may also have trouble learning to read. However, not all children with this history will experience difficulty.

7. **Children who have difficulty with *auditory processing* (also known as central auditory processing) may experience reading problems.** An auditory processing disorder is a neurological disorder that results in difficulty perceiving and understanding oral language despite having good hearing acuity. There are several types of auditory processing disorders. The diagnosis must be made by an audiologist in a sound-treated room.[15] These boys and girls have trouble perceiving and understanding what they hear. Children

> **Auditory processing disorder** is a neurological disorder that results in difficulty perceiving and understanding oral language despite good hearing acuity.

with auditory processing problems may have difficulty following directions because they do not understand what is being said. Often parents think this is a problem with memory. *However, it is important to recognize that children can't remember that which they never perceived or understood in the first place.* Others may interpret difficulty following directions as an attentional problem.

---

15   "Understanding Auditory Processing Disorders in Children," by T. J. Bellis, n.d. Retrieved from www.asha.org/public/hearing/understanding-Auditory-Processing-Disorders-in-Children.

However, children will become inattentive if they have trouble understanding and following what is said.

Check out your child's ability to follow a two-step direction. *Put this paper on the table, and then bring me the pencil.* Next, see if he can follow a three-step direction. *Hop across the room, stop and touch your toes, then put your hands on your hips.*

Educational indicators. There are several school indicators that can alert you to reading problems.

1. **Is your child in the lowest reading group?** If there are no reading groups, ask the teacher how your child's reading skills rank relative to other children in the class. Jacob's teacher said that she did not have reading groups. However, when Suzanne persisted, the teacher agreed that he was among the slowest in the class to pick up pre-reading and beginning reading skills.

2. **Does your child confuse letters and have trouble recalling letter names and letter sounds?** These are skills that should be in place by the end of kindergarten. Jacob did not learn all the sounds of letters until second grade.

3. **Does your child find it difficult to sound out words and tend to guess at words rather than sound them out?** Children should know how to sound out words at their grade level by the end of the first grade.

4. **Does your child overrely on story pictures to help figure out words on a page?** Jacob could not sound out words and used pictures on the pages to help him guess at words.

5. **Does your child overrely on the content of what he reads to help him guess at words?** There are two indicators that your child may be overrelying on content to help guess at words. These errors suggest that he may be re-reading and self-correcting based on new content information.

   • He frequently repeats words and phrases in the passages he reads.
   • He makes numerous self-corrections while reading.

6. **Does your child miss the same words repeatedly?** Some children have difficulty recalling a word from one line to the next because they have trouble sounding out words or they have difficulty with visual recall.

7. **Does your child have trouble with rote memorization?** Children who have trouble with rote memorization, such as learning multiplication tables or state capitals, may need context to help them learn. It is very hard for them to memorize isolated facts.

8. **Does your child drop off word endings or confuse the internal letters in words when reading?** For example, he may read "stopping" as "stop" or "interesting" as "interrupted."

9. **Does your child tend to skip lines when reading, combine words, omit words, or insert words that are not there?** For example, he may read, "we baked a cake" as "we baked a chocolate cake." He may read, "Dad said we had to find his owners because they would want him back" as "Dad said his owners would want him back."

10. **Does your child fatigue easily when reading?** Reading is an exhausting activity for struggling readers and they frequently become tired when reading.

HOW DO I DETERMINE MY CHILD'S READING LEVEL?

In 1996 the National Academy of Sciences (NAS) formed a committee of distinguished experts in the field of reading to investigate strategies for preventing reading problems. Their report, published in 1998, provides parents and educators with valuable information that remains relevant today. It outlines reading goals that a student should meet from kindergarten through Grade 3.[16] It is important to note that these goals are only guidelines because reading curricula vary from state to state and even among communities within the same state. Some states do not have mandatory kindergarten and do not begin formal reading instruction until the first grade. Other states require that children attend kindergarten.

> **ACT:** If you identify one or more marker in your child, it is time to become familiar with grade-level reading skills to determine if he is on track.

A summary of the NAS guidelines for kindergarten and grades 1, 2, and 3 is provided in this chapter. These are the reading skills that a student should possess by the *end of that school year.* These guidelines can help you determine whether your child's beginning reading skills are on target for his grade level.

---

16   *Preventing Reading Difficulties in Young Children,* by National Research Council (eds. C. Snow, M. Burns, and P. Griffin), 1998, Washington, DC: National Academy Press.

SUMMARY OF
NATIONAL ACADEMY OF SCIENCES GUIDELINES
FOR KINDERGARTEN

By the end of kindergarten, a student should be able to do the following:

▶ Write his first and last name.

▶ Write most letters and some words when they are dictated.

▶ Recognize and name all uppercase and lowercase letters.

▶ Provide the sound for most letters.

▶ Recognize some words by sight.

▶ Retell, reenact, or dramatize simple stories that are read to him.

▶ Correctly answer questions about stories read aloud.

▶ Identify single syllable words that rhyme.

▶ Produce a word that rhymes with another.

▶ Identify the beginning sounds in words.

▶ Break a spoken word into syllables.

▶ Use correct or invented spelling to write.*

▶ Listen attentively when an adult reads a story.

 * Invented spelling refers to the ability to correctly sequence the sounds in a word even if the word is spelled incorrectly. For example, c-a-t could be spelled as k-a-t or i-s could be spelled as i-z.

SUMMARY OF
NATIONAL ACADEMY OF SCIENCES GUIDELINES
FOR FIRST GRADE

By the end of first grade, a student should be able to do the following:

▶ Have a reading vocabulary of 300–500 words.

▶ Read aloud first grade fiction and nonfiction books with *accuracy and understanding.*

▶ Accurately read phonetically regular, one-syllable words and non-sense words (e.g., stop, cat, zot, thin, bush).

▶ Use letter-sound correspondence knowledge to sound out unknown words when reading text.

▶ Monitor own reading to self-correct mistakes and to understand what is read.

▶ Recognize by sight some common irregularly spelled words (e.g., have, said, where, is).

▶ Read and understand simple directions.

▶ Spell correctly three- and four-letter short vowel words (e.g., cat, sun, chin, let, shop).

▶ Create fairly readable first drafts using appropriate parts of the writing process (some attention to planning, drafting, re-reading for meaning, and some self- correction).

▶ Answer simple written comprehension questions based on material read.

▶ Use basic punctuation and capitalization.

SUMMARY OF
NATIONAL ACADEMY OF SCIENCES GUIDELINES
FOR SECOND GRADE

By the end of second grade, a student should be able to do the following:

▶ Accurately read and comprehend second-grade fiction and nonfiction books, recalling facts, details, and main ideas.

▶ Accurately decode words of more than one syllable at the second grade level (capital, Kalamazoo).

▶ Accurately read many irregularly spelled words and such spelling patterns as diphthongs, special vowel spellings, and common word endings.

▶ Be able to sound out unfamiliar words.

▶ Read voluntarily for pleasure.

▶ Correctly spell previously studied words and spelling patterns in own writing.

▶ Represent in correct sequence all sounds in a word when spelling independently.

▶ Produce a variety of types of compositions (stories, reports, correspondence).

▶ Reread sentences when meaning is not clear.

▶ Recall facts and details of texts.

SUMMARY OF
NATIONAL ACADEMY OF SCIENCES GUIDELINES
FOR THIRD GRADE

By the end of third grade, a child should be able to do the following:

► Read third grade level books with accuracy, fluency, and understanding.

► Sound out unfamiliar words.

► Read grade-appropriate chapter books of fiction independently.

► Summarize major points from fiction and nonfiction texts.

► Discuss the underlying theme or message when interpreting works of fiction.

► Ask "how," "why," and "what if" questions when interpreting nonfiction texts.

► Use information and reasoning to examine bases of hypotheses and opinions.

► Infer word meanings from taught roots, prefixes, and suffixes.

► Correctly spell previously studied words and spelling patterns in own writing.

► With some guidance, use all aspects of the writing process in producing own compositions and reports.

► Combine information from multiple sources in writing reports.

► With assistance, suggest and implement editing and revision to clarify and refine own writing.

► Produce a variety of written works (e.g., literature responses, reports, "published" books, semantic maps) in a variety of formats, including multimedia forms.

GUIDELINES FOR DETERMINING THE READING LEVEL FOR STUDENTS IN GRADES 4–12

Once children enter the fourth grade, there is no longer instruction in decoding as part of the mainstream curriculum. Students may have instruction in other language arts skills, such as vocabulary, grammar, and higher-level reading comprehension, but decoding skills are no longer taught. At this point students are expected to have well developed reading skills and be able to use those skills to learn new information in subjects such as social studies and science. What you really need to know at this stage is whether your child can read the grade-level material that is assigned in class and for homework. You will find instructions for how to determine whether your child can manage grade-level material in Appendix E.

If you have questions about whether your child is able to meet the standards outlined for his grade level, you can administer one of the informal screening tests found in the appendix of this book.

- ▶ Appendix A: Kindergarten Screening Test

- ▶ Appendix B: First Grade Screening Test

- ▶ Appendix C: Second Grade Screening Test

- ▶ Appendix D: Third Grade Screening Test

- ▶ Appendix E: Grades 4–12 Guidelines

These are informal screening tests written specifically for this book. They will help you determine whether your concerns are justified. These easy-to-administer tests are designed for parents to administer to their own children. They follow the grade-level skills outlined in the

NAS guidelines and the grade-level skills outlined in standards for each grade level by the Common Core State Standards.[17] Although these are not formal tests, they will give you a general idea of whether your child can manage grade-level reading material.

In addition to the copies of these tests in the appendices, you can visit *www.SmartKidCantRead.com* to download full-sized, ready-to-use versions of the tests. You will also find videos to watch that are linked to our website, where you can see professionals administering the tests. You may find it helpful to watch these videos before administering the test to your own child.

> **FACT: Common Core State Standards** provide guidelines for what every student should know and be able to do in math and English language arts from kindergarten through 12th grade.

If you find that your child has difficulty with the tests, *stop the testing*. Please do not become impatient with your child. Remember, he is doing the best he can. You have taken the first step, and now it is time for you to take the next one.

---

17   Common Core State Standards (Reading: Foundational Skills, Kindergarten), National Governors Association Center for Best Practices, Council of Chief State School Officers. National Governors Association Center for Best Practices, Council of Chief State School Officers, Washington D.C., 2010. Retrieved from www.corestandards.org/ELA-literacy/RF/K/,/1/, /2/,/3.

STEP TWO

Understand What Your Child Needs

CHAPTER THREE

GET AN INDEPENDENT EVALUATION

"Those who assess have a tremendous responsibility; assessment results are used to make decisions that directly and significantly affect students' lives."

—John Salvia and James E. Ysseldyke
Authors of *Assessment: In Special and Inclusive Education*[18]

When I first met Jefferson in my office, he had clearly given up. A good-looking, soft-spoken 13-year-old, Jefferson had been struggling with reading all his life. With a game expression on his face, Jefferson stumbled through the tests. He'd gone through many tests before, and had no faith that yet another evaluation would make any difference.

"I'm just waiting," Jefferson told me. "I'll leave school as soon as I can—when I turn 16."

It was clear that not being able to read had already deeply affected the course of Jefferson's young life. I followed Jefferson throughout the remainder of his school career. When we met during his senior year, he was smiling. He was about to graduate

---

18 *Assessment: In Special and Inclusive Education* (9th ed., p. xx), by J. Salvia and J. E. Ysseldyke, 2004, Boston, MA: Houghton Mifflin.

and had plans for continuing his education. He wanted to be a forest ranger.

What happened to change the course of Jefferson's academic career?

By the time Jefferson first came to see me, he had already been evaluated many times by his school system. An initial test in third grade indicated that Jefferson had low-average intelligence. His parents were advised to lower their expectations. Other tests in the fourth grade reported that Jefferson was reading at grade level and did not need any help. Despite being labeled an "average reader," he was put into a special reading remediation program in the fifth grade, and yet another remediation program in the sixth grade. A different reading program was tried each year by teachers who genuinely tried to help him—but nothing helped.

At one point his teachers concluded that he had attention-deficit disorder (ADD) and should be put on medication. When his parents resisted this suggestion, the school found other ways to "help" him.

By the seventh grade, Jefferson was placed in another special education program with 12 other students who also had reading problems. He started yet another reading program. He was mainstreamed for science and social studies, where a teacher's aide took notes for him in class. He listened to audio textbooks. He had no problem with homework because he had no homework! A teacher's aide "scribed" his answers for him on tests and written assignments. Everything was done to provide Jefferson with **accommodations** to help him "keep up" with the curriculum. But he really wasn't "keeping up." The *accommodations only helped him avoid reading and writing. He didn't need to read. All books, assignments, and tests were audio books or read to him. He didn't need to write. He dictated all assignments and test answers to a teacher's aide, who wrote the answers for him.*

His attorney later said, "Someone read for him. Someone wrote for him. He didn't even need to show up." (And he frequently didn't.) During all of this time, the school suggested that he was doing fine, getting A's and B's. His parents couldn't see how this could be possible since he didn't seem to understand the material.

> Educational **accommodations** are support services students receive to do *grade-level* work (e.g., listening to audio books). Educational **modifications** are changes that *alter* the content, instructional level, or performance criteria of the curriculum (e.g., third grade spelling words for a fifth grade student).

Jefferson's parents advocated for him for years. They were active and involved. They went to every team meeting together, trying to get improved services. Despite doing all they knew how to do, they were getting nowhere because they lacked the facts and documentation to back up their requests. They were not satisfied with the school's attempts; they knew that their son's prospects for the future would be very limited unless he learned to read. When Jefferson's parents took him to a private reading tutor, she told them that he needed an independent, diagnostic evaluation to provide them with information about Jefferson's strengths and weaknesses. They needed specific recommendations for reading help that were based on his diagnostic profile.

Finally Jefferson and his parents arrived in our office. This is what my reading evaluation told me about Jefferson:

Jefferson was a seventh grader who was reading at a third grade level. He was of average intelligence. He had a reading disability that could have been corrected years ago, but that had worsened after years of questionable testing and attempts at a series of different reading programs that did not meet his needs. His teachers were well-meaning and tried to help him, but he never had a teacher with appropriate training in helping students with reading problems.

Furthermore, he had given up and did not believe there was any point in trying any longer. But his parents had not given up. Based on his independent evaluation, Jefferson's parents began a lengthy legal struggle with the school system. He was eventually sent to a school that specialized in working with dyslexic students. Finally, placed in an appropriate environment with well-trained teachers, he learned to read.

A comprehensive, diagnostic evaluation, correctly administered, helped turn Jefferson's life around. The evaluation provided his parents with a road map to help them understand his strengths and weaknesses and offered specific recommendations to help him with learning in general and with reading in particular. Most importantly, his parents were willing to follow through and do what needed to be done to see that he learned to read.

"Everything changed when we went outside the school system," said Jefferson's father. "We finally learned what our son needed. Before, it was all about what the school had and what the school wanted to do. Once we had a professional to help us, it became about what our son needed."

Many reading problems are a direct result of inadequate instruction in the early grades when children first learn to read. Jefferson was a clear case of just such an "educational casualty." He had a mild reading disability that would most likely have responded to appropriate instruction when he first learned to read. In fact, his problem could possibly have been avoided altogether in a community where there was a strong reading program in kindergarten and first and second grade. The school's failure to address Jefferson's problems in the early grades inadver-

> **FACT:** Students who are "educational casualities" often suffer from inadequate reading instruction in the early grades.

tently resulted in a huge expense down the road for the school system and years of shame and feelings of failure for Jefferson.

To understand why the school's testing hadn't resulted in appropriate help for Jefferson, why all the school's attempts with different reading programs failed, and what Jefferson's parents could have done to help him earlier, you need to know what your school system can't tell you.

WHAT YOUR SCHOOL CAN'T TELL YOU

It is important to distinguish between reading tests administered by schools and an independent, diagnostic evaluation completed by a professional outside the school system. Schools are required by law to test to determine a child's eligibility for special education services. However, they seldom address the issue of *why* children have trouble with reading, or provide a diagnosis that effectively outlines a student's strengths and weaknesses.

Your school system is not a diagnostic facility. When a school evaluates your child for special education services, *the school is testing to see if your child qualifies under state law for special education help.*

The school does not provide a diagnosis. An evaluation by a trained diagnostician includes a comprehensive profile of your child's strengths and weaknesses. Few schools are equipped to do this. Without this information, they cannot provide appropriate recommendations that address a child's needs.

Although the federal law provides certain guidelines for identifying children with special needs, criteria for services actually vary from state to state. A student may, for example, qualify for special education help in Texas but move to New Hampshire and be "cured" overnight because he does not qualify under New Hampshire state law.

TIP: Your school system is not a diagnostic facility.

Your child may fall victim to the arbitrary nature of some state laws, such as the change of law that took place in Massachusetts. In 1998 the state determined that special education services were becoming too costly and too many children were receiving services—so they changed the law, with the result that fewer children qualified for services. That is, many children who received help with reading in 1998 no longer qualified in 1999.

Criteria can even vary from town to town or from one school district to another within the same state. More affluent communities usually have more money to spend on providing reading help than poorer communities. The benchmark is often different in communities where parents are well educated and have higher expectations for their children than in communities where parents are less well educated and where there is more poverty. There can even be differences in determining eligibility for services from school to school within the same town. These differences often depend on availability of trained staff and leadership in the student's school building.

I recently evaluated Tom, a fifth grade boy with significant reading problems. He lived in an affluent suburb. His school team decided that he no longer needed help and wanted to discontinue all his tutoring in reading. His parents knew that he was still reading several years below grade-level and suspected that a staffing shortage, not a change in their son's needs, prompted the team's decision. They went to the superintendent and requested a change of building. After considerable negotiation with the superintendent and director of special education, he was reassigned to a different school in the same town, where he received one-on-one tutorial help four times per week!

Tom's parents had done their homework. They understood their school system's politics and identified the reason that their team wanted to discontinue services—they no longer had a teacher available in his school to provide the one-on-one services Tom needed. Tom's parents had also identified a well-qualified reading teacher in one of the system's other schools. They recognized that the only person who could make the decision to change their son's school was the superintendent. An important point here: While speaking with the superintendent can sometimes be successful, it should *never* be your first step. Do your homework first, and consult with an advocate.

School systems rarely have experts who are trained in diagnostic evaluations. Few school systems have personnel with expertise in completing a differential diagnosis. For example, school personnel could not correctly identify the reason for Jefferson's inattention. They merely assumed it was due to attention-deficit disorder and did not investigate other possible causes for his inattention, such as anxiety, depression, an auditory processing disorder, or a language disorder.

School specialists you may encounter:

▶ **School psychologists** give intelligence tests and other tests that evaluate cognitive functioning.

▶ **Special education teachers** administer educational tests—math, reading, and written language.

▶ **Speech and language therapists** evaluate a child's oral language.

▶ **Occupational therapists** assess fine motor skills, like pencil grip.

▶ **Physical therapists** evaluate gross motor skills, like catching a ball.

In Jefferson's case, the school did not administer appropriate tests, nor did they know how to interpret the tests they administered. The district advised his parents that he was a slow learner and would always have trouble learning; he would probably never be a good reader. This was not the case. Jefferson was a boy of average intelligence. Later, the school concluded that he had attention problems and they were the reason he was having trouble learning to read. Again, this was not true. He was inattentive in class but not because he had attention-deficit disorder. Jefferson had given up and saw no point in school.

The school never made a correct diagnosis, and they never questioned their teaching methods. They were not able to correctly identify his intellectual ability because they did not have the staff to administer an appropriate intelligence test. No one actually evaluated him for ADD or for any other possible explanations for his inattention in the classroom. The school simply assumed that he had ADD because he was unmotivated and did not engage in classroom activities. The social-emotional factors that interfered with Jefferson's learning were never identified or addressed. In short, his school system failed to look at the whole child to evaluate his strengths and weaknesses and the cause for his struggle with reading. These types of errors in evaluations happen in all schools, from the most affluent to the poorest communities to all those in between. Schools simply do not have highly skilled diagnostic capabilities.

School systems often have limited resources. Few school systems have enough appropriately trained teachers to help all their children with reading problems. As a parent, you are actually competing with other parents for those resources! There are seldom enough to go around. It is essential that you become involved in advocating for services. *When I complete a program observation of a student I evaluate, I frequently*

> **FACT:** Recommendations for reading help should *not* be determined by local standards or available funding and staffing in a state or community.

see other children with equal or greater needs who are not receiving appropriate services—because their parents are not involved. Students frequently receive less help than they need because there are just not enough teachers to provide the help. Thus, reading help gets divvied up to the neediest, until these children show some improvement. Then their

> **TIP:** It takes a long-term commitment to get students to begin to improve and then to sustain and build on each gain.

reading help is removed so other students can begin to receive attention. The entire process is not designed to remediate successfully a reading problem, but to do what is possible with limited staffing. This type of "Band-Aid" approach will not have lasting, permanent effects and can leave children with chronic reading problems. It takes a long-term commitment to get students to begin to improve and then to sustain and build on each gain.

School systems frequently fail to provide appropriate reading support. Most school systems do not have enough teachers who are trained in evidence-based reading methods. As a result, they often use teachers who are not trained to help struggling readers. Some school systems persist in using inappropriate reading methods that do not result in improvement. Other school systems provide no help at all.

Jefferson's parents were very involved and met with their school frequently to advocate for improved services. None of the school's evaluations included specific recommendations of what he needed in terms of reading help—perhaps because the school did not have anyone trained in any of the appropriate programs or perhaps because they did not know what he needed.

The school provided a different reading program every year. There was no continuity from one year to the next. *Continuity of instruction is essential for a child's success. Children need to practice the same routines so that a skill set is established.* Switching programs disrupts the reading process, and students are not

> **WARNING:** When we provide students with the wrong type of help or insufficient help and they do not make progress, they come to view themselves as hopeless and unteachable.

able to practice until they have achieved mastery over the material.

The decision of what program to provide appeared to depend on availability of staff rather than Jefferson's actual needs. While Jefferson's

> **TIP:** Continuity of instruction is essential for a child's success. Children need to practice the same routines to establish a skill set.

teachers were well-meaning, none of the teachers who taught him had appropriate training to work with children with reading disabilities. At one point, the district did use an appropriate reading program, but the teacher was untrained in the use of the program. As a result, the school concluded "it did not work." Finally, both Jefferson and the school gave up. His teachers just provided him with support and accommodations to avoid the need to read or write. He was stuck and made no progress. Fortunately for Jefferson, his parents had not given up.

YOUR CHILD'S NEED FOR AN INDEPENDENT COMPREHENSIVE EVALUATION

A good, comprehensive diagnostic evaluation is a critical first step in determining whether your child has a reading disability. A diagnostic evaluation assesses your child's strengths and weaknesses and provides you with recommendations tailored to his individual needs. The evaluation should be based on established findings of reading research and must cover attributes we know to be associated with reading difficulties. This is *not* an arbitrary process and is *not* determined by local standards or available funding and staffing in a state or community.

A comparison with a medical diagnosis may help to make this point. What if you were diagnosed with cancer and were eligible for surgery and treatment under your current health insurance, but after changing insurance policies, you were no longer eligible for treatment? After some investigation, you discovered that the diagnostic criteria in your new policy required demonstration of a tumor of a larger size. Would this seem reasonable to you?

A good evaluation must be independent and free from the pressures to conform to budgetary and reporting constraints. Even when the school

> **TIP:** A good evaluation must be independent and free from the pressures to conform to budgetary and reporting constraints.

personnel administering the tests are skilled and beyond reproach, there is no way to get around the bias inherent in an evaluation administered by the school. This is not to assign blame; it is simply a reality and the nature of the situation. Jefferson, for example, did not receive the type of instruction that he needed to make improvement. Instead, he was provided with the instruction that was available by teachers who lacked the appropriate training. Year after year he endured inadequate, and often inappropriate, reading help. Of course he gave up; he needed to retain some self-respect.

An outside, unbiased evaluation should provide you with the information you need to understand your child's strengths and weaknesses. You need to become an expert on why your child is having trouble learning to read and what he needs to improve. You are the only constant factor in your child's educational life. Teachers change every year, school resources change frequently, and your child will change schools as he moves from elementary school to middle school to high school. Directors of special education and team chairpersons in your town come and go. You will always be there, making sure your child is making progress.

> **ACT:** Become an expert on your child's reading needs. Why is he having trouble learning to read? What does he need to improve?

You must learn to advocate for your child's services. Complete and accurate information is essential to your effectiveness. Obtaining test results and educational recommendations that are *unbiased* and *free* from budgetary and personnel concerns is essential. Understanding those results is key to knowing what direction your advocacy must take.

Recommendations for reading help are a critical part of an evaluation for children who struggle with reading. You need recommendations based on an accurate evaluation of your child's strengths and weaknesses. Unbiased recommendations come from an independent, professional evaluation. Schools are often caught in a conflict of interest. If your child requires a particular type of reading program, but your school does not have teachers trained in that type of program, would you expect them to recommend it? Not likely. If your child requires daily help in reading, but there are not enough teachers to provide that service, are they likely to recommend it? Probably not.

Yes, testing done by the school is free, and yes, I know the school told you there is no need for you to spend the money to get an independent evaluation. If you disagree with what the school proposes, you will need an independent evaluation to provide you with the necessary information and backup.

Federal law provides that the local school must pay for outside independent evaluations in certain circumstances when parents disagree with the school's test results. The implementation of that portion of the law varies from state to state. If finances are an issue, check with your local school system to learn the

> **TIP:** Unbiased recommendations come from a professional evaluation and are based on your child's unique needs.

procedure in your state and community. In some cases, public funding of an independent evaluation may depend upon family income. While schools are required to give you a pamphlet explaining your rights, they may not be quick to point out this funding option.

WHO SHOULD ADMINISTER EVALUATIONS?

The diagnosis of a reading disability is a complex process and must be done by a qualified and knowledgeable person. You need a professional who has experience with reading problems and who has the training and expertise to make appropriate educational recommendations. The individual must understand the relationship between reading and language. The person must know how to evaluate the differences among specialized reading programs in order to make appropriate recommendations. He or she needs to understand which tests to use and how to interpret test results. These are specialized skills that require years of training and experience. Schools seldom have the staff with this level of diagnostic training.

Such a person may be part of a clinic or in private practice. Evaluations can be done by teams of professionals or by a single individual. You can locate appropriate diagnosticians by contacting your local chapter of the *International Dyslexia Association* or the *Learning Disabilities Association*. Talk with other parents and ask them for names of professionals they have found helpful. Find out which diagnosticians will do classroom observations as part of the evaluation and which ones will accompany you to a team meeting to explain their results and recommendations to the team. Avoid popular tutoring chains that promise quick results. When speaking with diagnosticians as you search for one to assess your child, do not hesitate to ask questions. Here are some questions you want to ask:

▶ *What are your credentials?* You are looking for a professional with a doctoral degree (PhD or EdD) in learning disabilities, reading, psychology, or education.

▶ *What is your experience in evaluating reading problems?* Many psychologists specialize in specific areas. Make sure your professional has experience and expertise in working with reading problems.

▶ *What will your evaluation cover?* You want a professional who will provide a comprehensive evaluation by looking at your whole child. A comprehensive evaluation will look at your child's functioning in the following areas:

  • Intellectual and cognitive ability, including the evaluation of executive functioning

- Language ability
- Educational skill levels in reading, math, spelling, and written language
- Social/emotional functioning, including an evaluation of ADD if necessary
- Fine and gross motor skills, if necessary

> **Executive functioning** refers to a person's ability to plan, organize, carry out, and monitor purposeful cognitive activity.

▶ *How specific are your recommendations?* Vague recommendations will not be helpful. You need someone who is willing to make specific recommendations about the type of reading program required, how often your child needs help, and whether the help should be one-to-one or in a small group. This requires someone with knowledge of specialized reading instruction and intervention programs.

▶ *Will you attend a team meeting at my child's school to explain the results and provide recommendations for the team?* Parents always tell us their school team responds very differently when the evaluator attends the meeting. You are much more likely to receive the help that has been recommended if the evaluator is there to explain test results and reasons for recommendations. Some evaluators participate in team meetings via computer or phone.

> **TIP:** Your child is more likely to receive the recommended reading help when your independent evaluator attends the team meeting.

▶ *Will you observe my child in the school setting as part of the evaluation?* This is a valuable part of the evaluation. It provides the evaluator with firsthand knowledge about the current learning environment and what would help to improve the situation. Some evaluators may use a different professional to do the observation. The important issue is that the evaluator has accurate and objective information about your child's classroom functioning and learning environment.

▶ *Will you meet with me after the evaluation to discuss the results?* You need to become an expert on your child's needs. It is essential that you meet and are able to ask any question you may have. You need to fully understand your child's strengths and weaknesses and what he needs to help him learn.

▶ *What is the cost of the evaluation, and is it covered by insurance?* My experience is that insurance companies may cover the psychological portion of the evaluation but not the educational area. Some evaluators who do not take insurance will work on a sliding scale. Some charge more for attending school meetings, while others consider it part of the cost of the evaluation; it can be helpful to know this in advance. If your school district is paying for the evaluation, ask whether the evaluator will accept the district's rate.

ACT: Ask your insurance company which parts of a diagnostic evaluation are covered by your policy.

WHAT SHOULD BE COVERED IN A COMPREHENSIVE EVALUATION?

Your child will meet alone with the evaluator in a quiet room for several hours. This may take more than one session and may require that he miss part or all of a school day. There is no single test for the evaluation of a reading disability; your child will take many different tests that will provide a detailed picture of his underlying problem. Together, these tests will provide a close look at your child's strengths and weaknesses in reading, written language, and the higher thinking abilities (including attention, working memory, planning, and organizing) that are important for learning to read.

A good evaluator is able to assess not just the answers your child gives but also the manner in which your child processes test questions. This analysis of how your child processes information can be as informative—or even more informative—than your child's answers and scores. An experienced professional may use both formal and informal tests that have been proven over time to get an accurate picture of the child. The results of this comprehensive evaluation will then be used to create an effective plan that will help your child learn to read at school.

FACT: The *way* your child processes test questions can be just as informative as the actual answers he provides.

It was this information that Jefferson's parents lacked. They did not have an impartial professional evaluation of their son's reading problem and did not understand what he needed in order to learn to read. They knew only that the services the school was providing were not working. There can be many reasons for a child's struggle with reading. It is important for you to know what part of the reading process is most problematic for your child.

Overview of a comprehensive evaluation. Your child's comprehensive individual diagnostic evaluation should include the following elements, which are explained in more detail in the sections to follow.

- ▸ A **personal history** that includes a developmental, medical, behavioral, academic, and family history.

- ▸ A measure of general **intellectual functioning.**

- An evaluation of **cognitive processing** (language, memory, auditory processing, visual processing, reasoning, processing speed, and executive functioning).

- Tests of specific **oral language skills** related to reading and writing success, including tests of phonological processing, verbal memory, and rapid naming.

- **Educational** tests to determine how your child does in the basic skill areas of reading, spelling, written language, and math.

- An evaluation of **social/emotional functioning** when appropriate.

- **A classroom observation** completed by the evaluator or other professional.

- **Recommendations** based on your child's academic, cognitive, and psychological strengths and weaknesses.

Personal history. The first thing a good evaluator will do is ask you questions about your family and your child's growing-up years. He or she will want to know things like the kind of delivery you had, when your child first learned to crawl, whether he has been prone to ear infections, and how his language development progressed. The evaluator will also ask about the extended family and whether any members have struggled to read, look at your child's behavior, and ask about his experiences in school. There are many different types of profiles of children with reading problems. An experienced evaluator will begin to pull the pieces together that make your child a unique individual. Your child may have been slower than his peers in developing language but may have been on target for motor development. Or perhaps he had many ear infections when he first entered school and the alphabet was being taught.

Intellectual functioning. A good evaluator will give your child a test that will determine his general intellectual ability. Reading disabilities exist at all levels of intellectual functioning; many children with above-average intelligence have trouble with reading. Tests of intellectual ability provide us with information about how your child learns and solves problems. Knowing a child's intellectual potential gives us insight into what children are capable of doing as well as what kind of progress we can expect them to make.

> **FACT:** Developmental, medical, behavioral, educational, and family histories are an important part of the evaluation.

Cognitive processing. What does your child do when presented with a logic problem? Can he predict what picture will come next when given a series of patterns? Your child's ability to think through a scenario and put all of the pieces together to solve problems will provide another important clue to the underlying strengths and weaknesses that form his unique learning profile. Your evaluator will give him a series of tests that will provide insight into why he is having difficulty learning. A trained professional knows the *cognitive* areas that are associated with reading and will include those tests in the evaluation to help determine the cause and severity of your child's reading difficulty.

Social/emotional functioning. Both you and your child's teachers may be asked to fill out questionnaires that ask about your child's attention, behavior, and socialization. Your evaluator may also administer various projective tests that assess your child's ability to cope with situations and to maintain sustained attention.

Academic ability. In addition to these formal tests that give us a picture of how your child learns, your evaluator will want to know how he can perform in the academic areas of reading, written language, spelling, and math. These tests are also necessary as we seek to determine the exact nature of his difficulty. While these tests may be similar to tests your child might be given in school, they are important pieces of the whole picture that the

> **ACT:** Visit *www.SmartKidCantRead.com* for a list of tests that are used to evaluate each of these areas.

evaluator is putting together. We need these pieces of the evaluation to establish a baseline of academic achievement so we can measure his progress over time.

The areas just described are included in evaluations of all learning disabilities, but there are eight areas that are essential for children who are being evaluated for a reading disability.

Essential Portions of a Reading Evaluation

1. **Phonological awareness.** In order to be a good reader, your child needs to be able to clearly hear each individual sound that makes up our language. A good evaluator will give tests that will determine whether your child can hear and manipulate the sounds that we generally associate with letters.

   These particular tests will be given orally because they have to do with the *sounds* of our language. For example, can your child identify rhyming words? Can he tell which word in a series has a different beginning sound than the others? Can he identify the beginning, ending, and middle sounds in a word? Can he pull a simple word apart into individual sounds? Can he manipulate the individual sounds in a word by changing the sequence of sounds? For example, can he change "cat" to "mat" or "hit" to "hat"? All of these skills come under the category of **phonological awareness.**

Note that **phonological awareness** is not the same thing as **phonics**. While phonics involves associating *the specific sound with the actual letter on the paper,* phonological awareness deals simply with hearing the sounds of language. In the last few decades, there has been a large body of research emphasizing the importance of this ability for learning to read.

There are many phonological tasks that you can expect your child's evaluation to include, such as the ability to create rhymes, delete sounds from words, move sounds from one place in a word to another place, and pull words apart into their individual sounds. If your child displays a weakness in this area, the good news is that phonological processing skills can be taught to children. Many kindergarten and preschool programs currently provide sound instruction in this important skill.

> **Phonological awareness** refers to a child's ability to identify and manipulate units of oral language, such as the individual sounds in a word.

2. **Rapid naming.** Within the last few decades, researchers discovered that there is a relationship between your child's ability to quickly name sequences of letters, objects, or colors and the ability to read. In reading, we quickly scan letters on the page and interpret those "marks" into something that makes sense. In the same way, as a child scans blocks of colors and provides a name for each one, this test reveals how quickly his brain can absorb information about a symbol, state that information, and then move on.

A good evaluator will give your child a test of rapid naming in order to discover if the nature of his reading problem is related to precise visual scanning of letters and letter patterns. Again, this will help determine the type of reading remediation he will need.

3. **Verbal memory.** The ability to recall language both in context and outside of a context is important for reading. An example of evaluating language in context includes reading a short story to your child and asking him to retell the story. When the evaluator wants to determine how he does with language that is not in context, he will read him a *list* of words and ask him to repeat it. Some children have trouble recalling information presented in isolation, while others become confused by the complexity of language in context.

4. **Decoding.** This refers to your child's ability to read individual words and to sound out unfamiliar words quickly and correctly. Obviously, the ability to decode words is key in reading and is the strongest predictor of reading comprehension. It is difficult to understand the printed word if you cannot decode it. The majority of reading problems are due to trouble decoding. Decoding should be evaluated in several ways. It is important to analyze a student's decoding errors in each of the following areas.

> **Decoding** is the ability to translate print into speech by rapidly recognizing and analyzing printed words. This involves matching letters or letter combinations to their sounds and recognizing the patterns that make syllables and words.

   ▶ Lists of real words. Students should be asked to read lists of words. These lists are usually a combination of common sight words that your child encounters in typical reading books, along with words that he should be able to easily sound out. Word list reading is particularly important because it *removes the context.* Many students are able to guess at words by using the general context; word lists eliminate that possibility.

▶ Lists of nonsense words. Nonsense words are words that are not real but that follow English phonetic patterns. This test evaluates your child's ability to apply his knowledge of reading to new, unrecognized words. By reading nonsense words, your child will not be able to rely on other skills, such as guessing or recognizing memorized words. This test will purely reveal to the evaluator *whether he can decode unfamiliar words.* Note: Students who receive good instruction in a structured, phonics-based program usually show significant gains on this type of test, so it offers one way to monitor their progress in the reading program.

▶ Decoding in context. It is important to have students read paragraphs orally to evaluate their ability to read longer passages. Often their ability to read in context is different from their ability to read word lists. Some children do better when reading stories because they use the context to guess at words. Other children have more difficulty reading in context because they have trouble working with long passages of print or struggle to understand language as it becomes longer or more complex. An expert evaluator will look closely at your child's ability to read words in isolation as compared to his ability to read words in context. *This comparison is key to a reliable diagnosis.*

The evaluator should give a formal test of reading in context as well as listen to your child read his grade-level textbooks orally. It is most informative to have children read from their science or social studies textbook. These are books of nonfiction that students will need to be able to manage independently. It is possible to calculate the reading rate and percentage of decoding errors when reading grade-level material. It can sometimes be very useful to record a student while he is reading material he is expected to be able to manage for classroom assignments. Teachers are often shocked to hear how a student is actually reading when these recordings are played for them.

5. **Reading comprehension.** The whole purpose of reading is to be able to understand what we read. It is essential to determine whether a student can actually follow what he reads. Most students who struggle with reading have difficulty with decoding. However, there are some children who are able to decode accurately but have trouble with comprehension. Tests of reading comprehension usually require a student to read several paragraphs and answer a series of questions. Some tests require students to read passages aloud, and others require students to read silently.

Accurate decoding is necessary for good comprehension of what is read; this is particularly true as the student advances into the upper grades, where the reading becomes more difficult, and it becomes harder to predict or guess at words based on the context. Some students, particularly those with strong verbal reasoning ability, are able to use their background knowledge and the story content to piece together information—even though they might have had significant trouble reading the words in the text. Some students struggle so hard to sound out the words that it is not possible to reliably determine their reading comprehension. Other students, particularly those with language processing problems, have trouble understanding what they read as the sentences become longer and more complex. It is essential to sort out those issues.

Children with weak reading comprehension require a different type of help than those who struggle to decode words. Some students have trouble in both areas. They labor to sound out what they are trying to read and do not understand even what they are able to decode. If your child struggles to decode and to comprehend, he will need help in both of these areas.

Vocabulary is an important part of reading comprehension, and you can expect to see tests of vocabulary as part of the evaluation. The evaluator will want to know about your child's exposure to a variety of words and his ability to read these words and to associate them with the correct meanings.

> **Reading comprehension** is the ability to understand what is read. Students with weak reading comprehension require a different type of help than those who struggle to decode.

It is important to make a distinction between listening comprehension and reading comprehension. Listening comprehension requires that your child understand and can recall what is said. Reading comprehension is a more complex process and requires that a child be able to accurately read the material, understand what it says, and recall the information. While listening and reading comprehension are related, they are not the same. It is often the case that students who have trouble understanding what they hear may also have trouble understanding what they read. *Their problem is with understanding language, in both written and oral form.*

6. **Reading fluency.** Fluency in reading refers to the ability to read words accurately and automatically. In order to do well in school, your child needs to be able to read grade-level words automatically without long pauses or laboring over each individual sound. Some students learn how to sound out words accurately, but

they cannot read quickly enough to keep up with the demands of grade-level work. Reading fluency is measured by timing the child as he reads passages. Most reading fluency problems are related to trouble decoding.

7. **Spelling.** Spelling is the ability to represent what is spoken in written form. In the field, we refer to this as "encoding." When we spell, or encode, we put something *into* a code. When we read, or decode, we take words *out of* a code. Thus, spelling and reading are opposites. Spelling requires your child to translate individual sounds into letters.

> **Reading fluency** is the ability to read words accurately and automatically.

Spelling should be evaluated in three ways. First, the evaluator will want to see samples of your child's *unedited written work.* Second, he will be asked to take a dictated spelling test. Finally, he will be asked to produce a *writing sample* during the evaluation. This writing sample will be evaluated for skills in written language as well as skills in spelling. Many students do better on dictated spelling tests than on actual writing tasks. A good evaluator will know how to examine your child's spelling errors to gain insight into both spelling and reading problems. Children who have trouble with reading usually also have trouble with spelling. Many times a student will continue to be a poor speller even after successful reading remediation.

> **FACT:** Students who have trouble with reading often have trouble with spelling.

8. **Written language.** Your child's ability to express ideas in writing will form an important part of the reading evaluation. Students

who have difficulty expressing themselves verbally may also have difficulty expressing themselves in writing. This is often because of the trouble they experience organizing and formulating language. Students with spelling weakness often attempt to avoid writing because they know they will make spelling errors. A good evaluation of written language will take a look at your child's ability to organize paragraphs, correctly form sentences, use appropriate grammar, spell correctly, and include age-appropriate vocabulary.

The ability to create appropriately complex sentences is important. In other words, can your child create only simple sentences, or can he use a variety of sentence types that are appropriate for his grade? Can he take these sentences and organize them into logical paragraphs that fit together? Your child's writing is not only an important key to understanding how he expresses himself, but also provides clues to underlying problems with reading comprehension, decoding, and spelling.

> **TIP:** Your child's skills in written language can provide clues to underlying problems with reading comprehension, decoding, and spelling.

9. **Classroom observation.** This portion of the evaluation should focus on whether the classroom instruction—and any special reading instruction—meets the needs of your child. Is there coordination between the classroom reading program and the specialized reading program? A description of the reading instruction your child receives and your child's response to that instruction are an important part of the evaluation. A

description of his behavior in the classroom should be included. This section should also include a summary of teacher comments and a breakdown of the language arts curriculum the teachers are using.

EVALUATING READING FOR THE YOUNGER CHILD

As you have learned, the best time to help children who have trouble learning to read is when they are young and first encounter difficulty. While children in kindergarten and first and second grade have limited reading skills, it is still important to know how well they can decode and to determine the reason for their struggle in learning to read. You need to know whether they are having difficulty with phonological processing, decoding, fluency or comprehension.

> **TIP:** The experience and expertise of the diagnostician are key when assessing children in kindergarten, first grade, and second grade.

The experience and expertise of the diagnostician are key when evaluating young children because most tests are not set up to identify children at this early stage of reading. You need an evaluator who specializes in reading problems because the clinical experience and judgment of your evaluator are particularly important when assessing children at this beginning stage of reading.

Your evaluator will evaluate your child's oral language skills, with particular focus on verbal memory, listening comprehension, phonological awareness, and rapid naming. He will use both standardized and informal tests to analyze his pre-reading and early reading skills. He will use tests to discover how well your child can match letters with sounds to read at his grade level. Your child's spelling and beginning skills in written language will also be analyzed. The evaluator will write down exactly what your child says when reading (and may record it), examining his errors for patterns.

EVALUATING READING FOR THE OLDER STUDENT (FOURTH GRADE AND ABOVE)

The evaluation of reading problems for students in Grades 4–12 follows the format outlined earlier in this chapter. A key consideration for the evaluator when making recommendations lies in attempting to achieve a balance between a child's need to receive remediation for his reading and not missing class instruction that will result in falling yet further behind his peers.

The older student who continues to struggle with reading faces many challenges. Most schools generally stop providing reading instruction as part of the regular education curriculum by the fourth grade. While there may be instruction in the classroom for written language, spelling, vocabulary, or higher-level reading comprehension, decoding skills are no longer taught. Recall that most children who struggle with reading have difficulty decoding. This means that the older student whose reading skills are below grade-level no longer has the opportunity to benefit from classroom instruction in decoding *and* there is no longer a scheduled reading period that can be used to provide extra reading help outside the classroom. Finding time in students' schedules when they can be pulled out of class to receive the help they need becomes a serious challenge. To compound this dilemma, older students usually require a longer period of time than younger students to improve their reading skills and to catch up with their peers.

Older students with reading problems frequently begin to develop behavioral and emotional issues as a result of their frustration and lack of success. Many have already spent years trying to hide their problem. These serious emotional concerns can interfere with their ability to close their reading gap and may lead to destructive behaviors. Their emotional and behavioral issues need to be assessed and addressed.

Schools often begin to address reading problems of the older student with educational accommodations and modifications of expectations rather than providing reading remediation. It is important to determine whether your child requires both remediation and accommodations/modifications. Few teachers who teach above the third-grade level are trained to teach decoding. Special reading help must be provided outside the regular classroom. Often this help takes the form of trying to help those students meet the demands of the curriculum by assisting them with assignments and test preparation—rather than teaching them to read. Getting your child the reading help he needs becomes a serious challenge and requires determination and a full understanding of his educational needs.

WHAT SHOULD BE INCLUDED IN A REPORT?

After the evaluator completes the testing, he or she writes a report. The report is a critical document in your advocacy, and you must understand what is in that report. Your child's report should include all of the areas just discussed. You should expect to see a summary of developmental, medical, behavioral, family, and educational history. Physical, social-emotional, and language development should be reviewed. Family history of reading problems should be considered. Any contributing medical problems, such as congenital defects, seizures, and chronic ear infections, must be noted. A complete history of the educational problem should be discussed, along with a description of interventions that have been attempted.

The report should provide a clear analysis of your child's intellectual and cognitive strengths and weaknesses as well as an analysis of his academic strengths and weaknesses. A discussion of his social/emotional functioning is important for a complete picture of your child. You can expect to see a list of all tests given, along with a detailed analysis of your child's performance on those tests. Scores for all standardized tests should be provided, along with a discussion of your child's ability to manage the demands of the tests. The report should include specific recommendations based on your child's academic, intellectual, cognitive, emotional, and developmental needs. *Most importantly, the test results should lead to a unique analysis of your child's underlying problem, followed by a concrete plan based on current research that will help him learn to read.*

> **TIP:** It is essential that you understand what your child's evaluation report says so you understand his needs and can advocate for them.

The evaluator should meet with you to explain the findings, and then accompany you to the team meeting to explain the results and recommendations to all team members. This is a crucial piece of the evaluation. Many parents tell me that when the evaluator does not attend the team meeting, the report is often ignored and the recommendations are not always considered.

As you can see, the independent evaluation is crucial to the whole process of getting the reading help your child needs. It is vital that you identify the appropriate evaluator, move forward with the assessment, and get a full, detailed report. The next chapter will provide you with further tools for understanding the results of your child's evaluation.

CHAPTER FOUR

UNDERSTAND TEST RESULTS

"When you master this information, you will understand your child's test scores. You will be able to use information from objective tests to make decisions about your child's program. You may find that your expertise exceeds that of many special education team members. You will have the tools you need to change your child's life."

—Pam Wright and Pete Wright
Authors of *From Emotions to Advocacy:
The Special Education Survival Guide*[19]

Maria entered my office with a look of sheer exasperation on her face. She thrust a sheaf of papers into my hands and began to speak before I even had a chance to offer her a chair.

"I am not a stupid person," she began. "I work as an administrative assistant. I am highly respected in the workplace as someone who loves new learning and enjoys continuing education. Why do I always feel so dumb when it comes to understanding my daughter's school evaluations?"

---

19 *From Emotions to Advocacy: The Special Education Survival Guide* (p. 74), by P. Wright and P. Wright, 1992, Hartfield, VA: Harbor House Law Press.

It took me almost 30 minutes to convince this frustrated mother that her inability to understand her daughter's recent test results had nothing to do with her own intelligence level. To the typical parent, facing 8–30 pages of typed scores, bulleted points, and paragraphs full of technical jargon is akin to reading a report written in a foreign language.

If you have ever felt like Maria, you have come to the right place. After reading this chapter, you will be empowered to engage in a conversation about your child's educational evaluation from an informed perspective, whether looking at tests given at school or analyzing a professional report.

Understanding test results is crucial if you are to have a voice in advocating for the services your child needs. Evaluations completed by your school system are used to determine your child's eligibility for services under your state's law. Even children in private schools are eligible for services paid for by public school funds. Since schools have limited resources to provide help in reading and written language, it is important to know what your child needs and press for the interventions she deserves. Parents who know how to interpret test results are better able to function as a vital part of the solution in putting together an action plan

> **TIP:** Understanding your child's test results is crucial if you are to have a voice in advocating for the services your child needs.

that will lead to success. In order to help your child, you need to know her cognitive and academic strengths as well as the specific areas that require focused attention and help.

GENERAL SCHOOL TESTING

Schools perform many different types of tests. It is helpful to distinguish among them. This will enhance your understanding of how to use test results.

Screening tests. Most classroom teachers administer group tests to kindergarten and first grade students to red-flag those who might experience difficulty in learning to read. If you are notified by the teacher that your child has been identified for further testing, *keep in mind your journey has just begun.* A school does not alert parents of their concerns unless there is a clear indication of a problem. I strongly recommend that you follow through once you have been notified. The purpose of the initial screening is just that: to screen out those children who are clearly *not* at risk and keep those in the net who need to be watched. These test results can help determine the need for further diagnostic evaluations. They are the first step in building information to decide if a student is eligible for special education services.

Progress monitoring. If screening measures indicate your child falls below grade-level in one or more areas of reading, you should expect the teacher to closely monitor her progress with short, informal assessments in the classroom. Some **progress monitoring** tests are given every few weeks, while others may be given once or twice a year. Such tests are meant to provide insight into whether the teaching that is taking place in the classroom is having a positive effect on your child's ability to read. These tests are often administered by the classroom teacher as she works to help your son or daughter achieve **benchmarks**. These measures are meant for planning specific lessons to help your child achieve reading goals. As an involved parent, do not hesitate to ask your child's teacher how much progress she has made since your last parent-teacher meeting. Is she any closer to her benchmark? Has she achieved her learning goals?

While it is important to ask such questions, many parents express concern about the value of regular classroom progress monitoring. Many find that the results from such monitoring do not always match up with the results of diagnostic evaluations. Be careful about accepting these scores at face value.

Outcome tests. Also known as *high-stakes* achievement tests, outcome tests are state-wide tests administered to most

> **WARNING:** Results of classroom progress monitoring scores are often inconsistent with the information obtained by objective independent evaluators.

students at the end of certain grades and are used to compare a student's performance to his or her classmates throughout the state. It is important to keep in mind that such tests are not intended to provide specific information to develop an educational plan for your child. *The point of high-stakes testing is to provide a checkpoint*. High-stakes tests may be used to make decisions about moving to the next grade and may be a part of high school graduation requirements. It is also important to realize these test results are sometimes used to evaluate schools. Therefore, school officials are highly motivated to see all students pass.

DIFFERENT TYPES OF TESTS

▶ **Screening tests:** General tests used to screen out those who are not at risk for reading problems.

▶ **Progress monitoring:** Short, informal assessments used by teachers to determine whether classroom instruction is resulting in appropriate progress for at-risk students.

▶ **Benchmarks:** Goals that indicate expected progress for students at regular intervals.

▶ **Outcome tests:** State-wide or district-wide achievement tests given once a year to indicate a student's overall progress in relation to her peers.

(See Chapter 7 for a discussion of whether to allow test accommodations for your child on high-stakes tests.)

INDIVIDUAL READING EVALUATIONS

If screening measures indicate your child may be at risk for reading failure and she does not meet expected goals during progress monitoring, the teacher may suggest a formal individual reading evaluation or placement in a response-to-intervention program. The school's reading evaluation may include tests given by a speech and language therapist, school psychologist, and special education teacher. Your child will be removed from the classroom, and the tests will be administered individually. The results of this evaluation form the basis for planning what will happen at school to help your child meet with success in reading.

Two types of tests are given in an individual evaluation:

1. **Criterion-referenced tests** (sometimes called informal tests) determine whether your child has grasped very specific information and skills. Rather than compare your child's performance to the performance of others of similar age and grade, *criterion tests let you know what your child can do.* For example, Holly has learned 13 out of 26 letter names. We now know exactly what Holly can do and where she needs help.

2. **Standardized tests** (sometimes called norm-referenced tests) must be administered by trained professionals who follow standardized procedures. These tests provide scores that *compare your child's performance with that of other students across the country who are at the same age or grade level.* For example,

Holly's performance was at the 31st percentile on a reading test. This means we are comparing Holly's score to other students across the country in her grade. *Thus Holly scored higher than 30% of children in her grade, and 69% of the students outranked Holly.*

Criterion-referenced tests: Informal measures of what your child can do.

Standardized tests: Formal assessments that compare your child's performance with the performance of students across the country of the same age or grade-level.

INTERPRETING STANDARDIZED TEST SCORES

It is particularly important to understand your child's test scores on standardized tests. These scores will provide the backbone of your plan. The total number of correct answers on a **standardized** test is called the **raw score**. This score is translated into a number of different terms in order to compare your child's reading ability with others in the same grade and age range. Just when you think you have one type of score figured out, we provide you with a new slant on things! Don't give up! Read this section of the book slowly, getting one new term down before you move on to the next. Refer back to these pages every time you review your child's formal testing.

The first thing an evaluator will do after scoring your child's tests and getting a "raw score" is to convert the "raw score" into a **standard score**. A standard score is simply the new name for a transformed raw score. Why go to all this trouble to come up with a new number for the raw score? *By using standard scores, evaluators are able to describe a student's performance compared to other students of the same age or grade level from across the country.*

Raw score: Total number of correct answers on a test.

Standard score: Name for a transformed raw score, used to compare a student's performance to others of the same age or grade.

Once we have the standard score, what comes next? Evaluators like to look at how the *average* student performs so they can determine how your child is doing compared to what you might expect. The **mean** score is the *average* score obtained by students of similar ages and grades taking the same test.

Standard deviation is a term evaluators use to talk about how much higher or lower a child is doing compared to the mean (average score). It is a standardized measure of how far above or below the average score your child's standardized score lies. That is, it tells us, given how all children's scores cluster around the mean, how far away from the mean your child's score falls. The majority of students fall within 1 standard deviation above or below the mean. *In general, if your child is more than 1.5 standard deviations below the mean, it's time to get worried.* Either your child was having a bad day when she was taking the test, or she needs some significant help in the area being tested.

Mean score: *Average* score obtained by students of similar ages and grades taking the same test.

Standard deviation: A measure of how far away from the mean score the student's standard score lies.

The mean standard score for most educational and psychological tests is either 10 or 100. When a test's *standard score has a mean of 10, the standard deviation is usually 3.* Now let's walk through the steps you just learned. If the *standard score* has a mean of 10, that means we are looking at an average of 10. If the *standard deviation* is 3, we are going to subtract 3 from 10 in order to get 1 standard deviation below the mean. Subtracting 3 from 10, we get 7. Thus, 7 is 1 standard deviation below the mean. A child with a standard score of 7 is performing in the low-average range. A score that is 1.5 standard deviations below the mean is between 5 and 6. This is below average and an area of serious concern. Parents of a child with a standard score of 6 or lower have cause for worry.

Now let's look at a test with a standard score that has a mean of 100. When a test's standard score has a *mean of 100, the standard deviation is usually 15.* Are you catching on? How are you going to calculate 1 standard deviation below the mean? Simply

> **TIP:** If your child is more than 1.5 standard deviations below the mean, it's time to get worried.

subtract 15 from 100. If a child receives a standard score of 85, she is performing 1 standard deviation below the average, or in the low-average range. However, a child with a standard score of 75 is more than 1.5 standard deviations below the mean. Now it is time to be concerned.

Let's take a look at how this plays out with a specific test. The Woodcock-Johnson IV (WJIV) is a standardized test battery with many individual tests that is often used by schools and evaluators to test reading. This test has a mean standard score of 100 and a standard deviation of 15. Let's assume that Holly received a standard score of 70 on the Letter-Word Identification test (a test of word list reading) on the WJIV. How many standard deviations below the mean is this? Remember that the standard deviation is 15. Thus Holly's score of 70 is 30 less than 100 or *2 standard deviations below the mean.* We have cause to be concerned about Holly's ability to read words.

On the other hand, Holly received a standard score of 115 on the Passage Comprehension test of the WJIV (a test of her comprehension of sentences); this score is 15 points or *1 standard deviation above the mean* and is in the high-average range. We have discovered a relative strength for Holly. While she struggles to read words, she is able to overcompensate by using her strong verbal reasoning ability to find the meaning of the passage.

Holly achieved a standard score of 85 on the Sentence Reading Fluency test (a test of her ability to read sentences fluently). This score is 15 points or *1 standard deviation below the mean* and is in the low average range. This tells us that she is a slow reader. You can see her scores displayed in Table 4.1.

Table 4.1 Holly's Standard Scores and Standard Deviations

TEST NAME	STANDARD SCORE	STANDARD DEVIATION
Letter-Word Identification	70	-2.00
Passage Comprehension	115	+1.00
Sentence Reading Fluency	85	-1.00

Now that you understand standard score, mean, and standard deviation, let's take a look at some of the ways evaluators like to look at test scores. The **percentile rank** for Holly is the percentage of people who score *at or below* Holly's standard score. Let's look at our previous example of Holly's standard score of 70 on the Letter-Word Identification test of the WJIV. This score is at the 2nd percentile. That means that 98% of the population scored better than Holly on this test. This is cause for serious concern.

Take a look at Holly's score on the other tests in our example (Table 4.2). You will remember that Holly achieved a standard score of 115 on the Passage Comprehension test of the WJIV; this score is at the 84th percentile. This tells us that Holly has scored higher than 83 percent of the population. Her standard score of 85 on the Sentence Reading Fluency test is at the 16th percentile. This tells us that Holly scored higher than 15 percent of the students at her grade level. What can we conclude? Based on these scores, it appears that Holly has significant difficulty reading words that are not in context and her reading is slow. On the other hand, while Holly may struggle to read, she has strong verbal reasoning ability and is good at guessing at words based on the general content of what she reads.

> **Percentile rank** is the percentage of students scoring at or below the student's standard score.

Table 4.2 Holly's Percentile Ranks and Standard Scores

TEST NAME	STANDARD SCORE	PERCENTILE RANK
Letter-Word Identification	70	2
Passage Comprehension	115	84
Sentence Reading Fluency	85	16

Percentile ranks provide parents, evaluators, and educators with a good representation of test performance that is easy to understand. If you are having trouble understanding test results, ask your evaluator to give you the percentile ranks for all standardized test scores. Make sure your evaluator provides you with the standard score and percentile ranks for *each* standardized test that was administered.

Now let's look at **age-equivalent (AE)** and **grade-equivalent (GE)** scores. An AE score tells us that a student's raw score on a test is *equivalent to the average score for students at that age level.* The AE is calculated in years and months. GE score tells us that a student's raw score on a test is *equivalent to the average score for students at that grade-level.* This is also calculated in years and months.

Age-equivalent score: Equivalent to the average score for students at that age level.

Grade-equivalent score: Equivalent to the average score for students at that grade level.

Look at Holly again, who is 12 years and 11 months old and in the seventh grade. Holly's score on the Letter-Word Identification test is equivalent to the average score for students who are 8 years, 1 month old. Thus, Holly's score can be written as AE = 8.1. This is one more way to realize that we have cause for concern. Her grade-equivalent score is equivalent to the average score for a student who is in the eighth month of the second grade (GE = 2.8).

Now that you understand what these scores mean, here is a general rule of thumb. *Grade-equivalent and age-equivalent scores need to be used very cautiously. These scores do not*

> **TIP:** Percentile rank scores provide a good representation of test performance that is the easiest to understand.

carry the same level of accuracy and precision as standard scores and percentile ranks, but they will give you a general sense of how your child is performing. Many parents find that *percentile scores* are the most helpful and easiest to understand.

NORMAL DISTRIBUTION

A term frequently encountered in the educational arena is the normal distribution of scores (also referred to as the bell curve). This means that when you test a group of people and plot their scores, those scores form a bell-shaped line graph (see Figure 4.1). The bulk of the scores cluster in the middle (around the mean). Remaining scores taper off evenly on either side (high and low). Scores with this distribution shape

> **Normally distributed scores** form a bell-shaped curve on a graph, indicating that most scores cluster in the middle around the mean. Remaining scores taper off evenly on either side (high and low).

are called **normally distributed**. The bell curve is simply one more way of looking at scores. By viewing scores graphically, we can visually grasp the relationship among a test's mean, standard deviation, standard scores, and percentile ranks.

Figure 4.1. The Relationship Among Scores

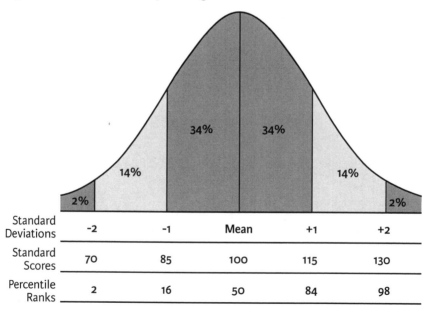

Standard Deviations	-2	-1	Mean	+1	+2
Standard Scores	70	85	100	115	130
Percentile Ranks	2	16	50	84	98

Figure 4.1 provides a visual display of the relationship between standard scores, standard deviations and percentile ranks. We can observe, for example, that a standard score of 85 is 1 standard deviation below the mean and is at the 16th percentile. A standard score of 115 is 1 standard deviation above the mean and is at the 84th percentile.

We can see that 2% of the test takers achieve a score of 2 or more standard deviations below the mean, and 2% of the populations achieve a score of 2 or more standard deviations above the mean. We can also see that 14% of the population achieve scores between 1 and 2 standard deviations below the mean and 14% achieve scores between 1 and 2 standard deviations above the mean. The majority of the population's scores cluster around the mean. Thus 68% of the population's scores range between 1 standard deviation below the mean and 1 standard deviation above the mean.

Most evaluators present their test results in a table such as Table 4.3. If you look at Figure 4.2, you can see that the same test scores are mapped out on a bell curve.

Table 4.3. Holly's Scores on the Woodcock-Johnson IV

TEST NAME	STANDARD SCORE	PERCENTILE RANK
Letter-Word Identification	70	2
Passage Comprehension	115	85
Sentence Reading Fluency	85	16

Figure 4.2 Holly's Scores on the Bell Curve

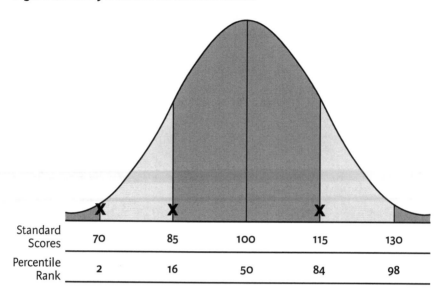

Standard Scores	70	85	100	115	130
Percentile Rank	2	16	50	84	98

You can see that mapping scores on the bell curve is just another way of presenting scores. It is a more graphic display of scores and you may find it very helpful to map your child's test scores on this bell curve each time you receive an evaluation report containing standard scores and percentile ranks. This will provide you with a visual display of your child's scores. It is eas-

> **ACT:** Print additional copies of the bell curve to plot your child's scores from our website: www.SmartKidCantRead.com.

ier to see how her scores compare to the average score when you map them out. Keep additional copies of the bell curve on hand.

Are you beginning to understand the relationship between standard scores, percentile ranks, and standard deviations? While this has been a technical section, it should help you to no longer feel "on the outside" as you enter conversations about your child's performance.

COMPOSITE OR CLUSTER SCORES

One more way of looking at a child's performance is to *combine* individual test scores to create **composite scores or cluster scores**. As a parent, you need to be wary of cluster or composite scores. *These scores are useful only when all the test scores within the cluster are similar. They can be misleading when the scores on the tests within the cluster are not similar.* While some school systems use cluster or composite scores, they should not be used to determine a student's eligibility for help with reading when the scores of the individual tests within the cluster are too far apart. Be sure that the evaluator has not overlooked your child's strengths or weaknesses by relying on a cluster score.

Let's go back to our example of Holly to see how this might happen. You'll remember that Holly scored at the 2nd percentile and had a standard score of 70 on the Letter-Word Identification test. This

> **WARNING: A composite or cluster score** is a score that results from combining individual test scores. Composite scores can be misleading when the scores on individual tests within the cluster are not similar.

test measured Holly's ability to read individual words. This score tells us that Holly has significant trouble decoding words.

On the Sentence Reading Fluency test, Holly scored at the 16th percentile, with a standard score of 85. You will remember that this is 1 standard deviation below the mean. This score suggests that Holly's reading is slow.

On the Passage Comprehension test, however, Holly scored at the 85th percentile, with a standard score of 115. You will recall that this is 1 standard deviation above the mean, suggesting that Holly has a good understanding of what she reads.

Evaluators may combine these three scores to create a composite score called Broad Reading. Are you following what will happen here? *Holly's Broad Reading score is going to be misleading because the combined scores do not tell the whole story!* Since Holly's performance is very different on the three tests, her Broad Reading score tells us nothing about her actual reading ability! If we use her Broad Reading score, Holly will appear to be a low-average reader and will not qualify for help. In reality, she is a weak reader who is good at guessing at meaning.

A good evaluator will analyze *individual scores* in order to make accurate conclusions about Holly's strengths and weaknesses. We can see that she has weak decoding skills and reads slowly. She does not appear to have trouble with reading comprehension. In fact, she appears to use her strong verbal reasoning ability to help her gain meaning from what little she can read of the passage. We will administer other tests to check

> **TIP:** A good evaluator will analyze *individual* scores in order to make accurate conclusions about a student's strengths and weaknesses.

out this hypothesis. Such an analysis will lead to an effective program for helping Holly in the exact areas where she needs remediation.

SIGNIFICANTLY DIFFERENT SCORES

You may hear teachers or evaluators talking about "significantly different scores." What does this mean and why is it important? A good evaluator is trying to get a composite picture of your child. Thus, *the evaluator will look at your child's scores relative to your child.* In other words, if your child tends to be high in many areas, the area that dips lower suddenly stands out. A good evaluator is like a scientist. He or she is curious, and wants to know not only what your child has scored but also how she processes questions, what methods and strategies she uses to answer questions, and how her scores relate to the whole. An evaluator who is sensitive to all of these issues is able to look at your child holistically, forming a balanced picture of what is happening that leads to the results on the individual subtests.

Remember a score that is 1.5 standard deviations or more above the mean suggests that this is an area of strength for your child. A score that is 1.5 standard deviations or more below the mean suggests that this is an area of weakness. Good evaluations should break down composite scores, homing in on areas where your child is strong and explaining specific areas needing help. If your child scores very high in one area and very low in another, this can be a strong clue as to why she performs the way she does in school. *Whenever you see variability, it is important to ask questions about the meaning of the scores in relation to one another.* You'll remember that Holly had trouble on the Letter-Word Identification test, yet did well when it came to Passage Comprehension. Based on observations of her performance during the test as well as her scores on other reading tests, a good evaluator will be able to explain why that might be and the implications for providing help in the classroom. Holly's score of 2 standard deviations **below the mean** on the Letter-Word Identification test stands out in

TIP: Question the meaning of any variability in your child's test scores.

stark contrast to her score of 1 standard deviation **above the mean** on the Passage Comprehension test. This is a difference of 3 standard deviations! Scores separated by at least 1.5 standard deviations make a significant statement about how your child is performing and should always be explained in the report. Whenever you catch this pattern, be sure to speak up. You need to know what is happening, why, and what can be done about it.

MEASURING YOUR CHILD'S PROGRESS

As a parent, you want to know whether your child is making progress in achieving the skills she needs to be a successful reader. Be sure to keep a file from year to year containing all test results. In order to make comparisons and track progress, test makers of some standardized educational tests have created alternate versions of the same test. If your child's team or independent evaluator feels it is time to take another look at her reading skills, it is possible to administer an *alternative* version of a test at any time. An evaluator may readminister the *same* version of a standardized test after 12 months.

When comparing this year's scores to previous evaluations, remember that it is always best to avoid using grade- and age-level equivalents. While your child may show improvement, her peers have also continued to develop their skills. The best way to monitor progress is to readminister the same standardized test to compare this year's test results with last year's test results. Use the *standard score and percentile ranks to determine whether your child has made progress.* By comparing your child's *standard scores and percentile ranks from one year to the next* you will know whether the gap is closing between your child's performance and the performance of her peers.

Once again, let's take a look at Holly. If her performance on the Letter-Word Identification test

> **TIP:** Monitor yearly progress by readministering the same standardized test. Compare your child's **standard scores** and **percentile rank** to determine whether the gap is closing between her performance and that of her peers.

improved from the 2nd percentile (standard score of 70) to the 16th percentile (standard score of 85), we know that she has made significant gains in her ability to read and sound out words. On the other hand, her ability to comprehend sentences has dropped from the 84th to the 81st percentile. While this is not a significant drop and could be due to chance, it is nonetheless in the wrong direction. Similarly, her reading fluency dropped from the 16th to the 15th percentile. It is possible that while Holly has improved in her decoding skills, her reading skills are not yet automatic, which causes her reading to remain slow. Her slight drop in comprehension might also be related to her increased focus on decoding accuracy. We will need to administer other reading tests to check out this hypothesis.

Table 4.4. Holly's Progress Monitoring

	APRIL 24, 2015		APRIL 29, 2016	
TEST	STANDARD SCORE	PERCENTILE RANK	STANDARD SCORE	PERCENTILE RANK
Letter-Word Identification	70	2	85	16
Passage Comprehension	115	84	113	81
Sentence Reading Fluency	85	16	82	15

It can also be helpful to use **criterion-referenced tests** when you are examining your child's learning trend. You will remember that this type of test measures your child against a *particular standard*, rather than against other students.

For example, Robert has learned eight additional letter names during the 6 week grading period. We now know what Robert can do compared to what he was able to do earlier. Criterion-referenced tests can be important for showing the progress your child is making. By looking at the scores, you will know the specific skills he has mastered over a period of time. However, criterion-referenced tests provide no information about how your child's performance compares with the performance of other children in the same grade.

THE USE OF TEST SCORES

Now that you understand a bit more about interpreting test scores, remember that *test results are not an end in and of themselves.* The purpose of putting your child through a process of evaluation is *not* to create a detailed sheaf of papers that look nice in a file. Remember that tests are useful only if they pinpoint what your child needs, how she will best learn to read, and what measures will be taken to insure her success. A diagnostic evaluation should lead to instruction that works. This involves making decisions about the type and amount of assistance your child will receive. The determination of services is based on the results of the evaluation and the recommendations in the evaluation reports.

> **TIP:** A diagnostic evaluation should lead to instruction that works.

At this point it is important for you to understand the science of reading. In order for you to make informed decisions about what is best for your child, you need to know how good readers learn to read and what works for those who struggle.

STEP THREE

Learn About
the Reading Process

CHAPTER FIVE
THE ABCs OF READING

"Skillful reading is not a unitary skill. It is a whole complex system of skills and knowledge."

—Marilyn Jager Adams
Author of *Beginning to Read:*
Thinking and Learning About Print[20]

As the mother of a precocious 6-year old, Serita described reading as a magical process. "Just provide your child with plenty of books," she told her friends. "That's all it took for my little Elena to catch on to reading. It all happens automatically in the right setting. Read to your child every night. Fill her room with books."

When Serita's second daughter was born, she entered parenting confidently. That's when the bubble burst. "I don't understand," she lamented in my office on a cold December morning. "Everything that worked with Elena has no effect whatsoever on Diana. She is very smart and a natural artist, but now her teacher is telling me that she is going to have to repeat first grade because she can't read. I was so unprepared

---

20   *Beginning to Read: Thinking and Learning About Print* (p. 3), by M. J. Adams, 1990, Cambridge, MA: MIT Press.

for this. I provided her with plenty of books and read to her every night, just like her sister. She always had trouble sitting still when we read to her, but I never thought that she would have trouble reading. What has gone wrong?"

HOW DO GOOD READERS READ?

Recall that reading is a skill that is related to a child's oral language ability. However, learning to read is much more complicated than learning to speak. Although most children pick up oral language naturally, reading is a complex skill that requires a number of processes to fall into place simultaneously. In order to start reading, a child must first be able to *hear* the separate sounds in a word. The ability to rhyme is an early indicator that a child is beginning to distinguish the separate sounds that make up words. This is one of the most basic pre-reading skills.

By the time a child enters kindergarten, we can expect her to be adept at learning to rhyme. This is the earliest indicator that she is developing phonological awareness, a skill that is key to success in reading. As you learned, phonological awareness refers to the ability to distinguish and manipulate individual sounds in words. As children move up the ladder, they progress from rhyming words to recognizing initial sounds in words, to pronouncing words without some of the sounds, to moving the sounds around.

As this solid foundation of phonological awareness is being built, a child must also learn to visually associate letters with the sounds. This is called **phonics**. Good readers begin by associating sounds with letters. They learn to blend those sounds into words and become very efficient at reading words and recognizing common letter patterns. A young child learns to recognize a word automatically after several repeated exposures to the word. As children mature neurologically and develop more reading skills, reading becomes increasingly automatic.

When a good reader encounters an unfamiliar word, she will sound it out. Good readers do not repeatedly guess at words they can't decode based on the content of what they are reading or based on the pictures in the book. While good readers may occasionally use the content of what

> **FACT:** Reading becomes an unconscious and automatic process for good readers.

they are reading to guess at the meaning of a word, they do not use guessing as a strategy to compensate for poor decoding skills.

THE BRAIN AND READING

Reading is a complicated process that involves several specific parts of the brain, now identified by researchers as the reading circuit.[21] The whole process begins as the brain breaks down the difficult job of reading into easier, more simplified jobs. These easier tasks are then sent off to different parts of the brain, where in-depth work occurs in specialized areas. The real beauty of it all lies in the connections between all these different parts of the brain, resulting in the wondrous process of reading!

For example, the very back of your brain, called the **occipital cortex**, is involved in visually processing the print of what you read. This is where you take in the actual words and letters printed on the page.

In the front of the brain, your frontal lobe, or **neocortex**, helps you find meaning in what you read. While the back of your brain is taking in the actual letters on the page, the front of your brain is working on translating those marks into something that makes

---

21 "Neuroimaging studies of language development reading and reading disabilities" by Kenneth R. Pugh, PhD. 2015. Retrieved from http://www.ortonacademy.org/cms/uploads/aogpe-2015-pugh-talk.pdf.

sense. In this neocortex, your brain processes the meaning of the words and sentences you read and connects what you are reading with what you already know.

But that's not all! While the back of your brain is interpreting the visual marks and the front of your brain is assigning meaning, the middle portion of your brain is working on translating all of this into speech sounds. Your **temporal lobe** processes the sounds associated with the letters and words you read. While there are many other tasks and parts of the brain involved, these are the three main functions and areas of processing. You can see that reading is no small task!

Scientists are able to take pictures of brain activity when an individual reads by using **MEG** (magnetoencephalography) or **FMRI** (functional magnetic resonance imaging). These pictures give us information about which parts of the brain are activated when we read.

Researchers who study the brain functioning of those who struggle with reading have found that there are two main differences in the brains of dyslexic individuals. First, the *structure* of the brain appears to be somewhat different in many individuals who have difficulty with reading. Second, studies have found that *different parts of the brain are activated* in those who struggle to read.

> **FACT:** Successful reading remediation changes brain activation patterns of struggling readers so their patterns begin to look more like those of successful readers.

For example, a struggling reader may rely more on the parts of the brain that break down word parts, while proficient readers are able to rapidly store patterns in the visual portion in the back of their brains.

Research has shown that when struggling readers are successfully remediated their brain activation patterns begin to look more like those of successful readers. Effective reading instruction actually changes brain activation patterns in the struggling reader.

INTELLIGENCE AND READING

Sadly, when children see their classmates struggling to read, they often believe that they are not as intelligent as the others. The child who struggles to read also commonly believes that he is "stupid" and cannot learn. This belief and the attitudes of fellow classmates can lead to the erosion of self-esteem and behavioral problems.

Children at all levels of intelligence can have trouble reading. We know that many children of average or above-average intelligence have trouble with reading. It is important to note that reading problems are not equivalent to low intelligence. While a struggling reader

> **FACT:** Reading problems exist at all levels of intelligence and do not imply low intelligence.

may be capable of complex thought, it is the vehicle by which she receives or conveys information that results in the breakdown. A child may readily grasp the implications of the events leading up to World War II, but if she can't read her textbook, we may assume she is incapable of understanding the information. Similarly, if she has difficulty writing, she may have difficulty conveying her level of understanding.

READING PROBLEMS AS PART OF A CONTINUUM

Some children learn to read with ease because they are able to automatically internalize the letter/sound associations. These children easily begin to apply phonics principles for automatic letter pattern and word recognition. Like Elena in our opening illustration, you may know some children who learned to read before entering kindergarten.

These students make any reading program look good because they learn to read regardless of the reading methods used. Often they had exposure to reading at home and generally love books. Their brains are able to perform the specific tasks required for reading with little or no explicit instruction. These children usually come from homes where the adults in their lives have read to them extensively. However, most of our school-aged population needs explicit teacher instruction in order to "crack the code" for reading.

Children vary greatly in their ability to acquire reading skills. Think of children as being on a *continuum* of learning, ranging from those who will learn to read prior to entering kindergarten, to those who will learn quickly with good instruction, to those who will experience difficulty and require specialized instruction. Even those who require specialized instruction vary in the level of severity of their problem.

> **FACT:** Reading problems exist on a continuum of severity.

More than half of our student population will require a structured, phonics-based reading program in kindergarten, first grade, second grade, and third grade if they are to become proficient readers. However, with appropriate teaching in the early grades, most children will become good readers. But a certain percentage of children on the severe end of the continuum will likely require special reading help to become good readers—regardless of the reading curriculum used in the early grades.

LABELS FOR READING PROBLEMS

Don't worry if you are confused about labels that are used for children who struggle to read. Most professionals are confused, too! This is because there is disagreement in the professional community about the definitions for these terms. Let's consider a few commonly used labels.

A **learning disability** is a **neurological disorder** that is caused by differences in brain structure or brain functioning, which leads to difficulty with specific types of learning. A learning disability interferes with the ability to process, store, or produce information and can affect the ability to read, write, speak, or do math. Again, there is disagreement in the professional community about the percentage of individuals who have a learning disability, but the estimates range from 5% to 20% of the school-aged population. In a classroom of 25 students this means between one and four children may have some type of a learning disability. Some people with learning disabilities also have coexisting disorders, such as attention-deficit disorder or difficulties with social interaction. Attention-deficit disorder is not a learning disability, although it can affect learning.

> A **learning disability** is a neurological disorder that is caused by differences in brain structure or brain functioning which leads to difficulty with the ability to process, store, or produce information.[22]

Think of the term "learning disability" as a general category that relates to a variety of tasks that involve the way a child's brain handles information. For the purposes of classification, the *Individuals with Disabilities Education Act of 2004 (IDEA)*, the law governing special education, places children with reading problems into this broad category. Children who exhibit difficulty with reading are classified as having a "specific learning disability" unless they also have other developmental issues that interfere with their learning.

---

22   Cortiella, Candace and Horowitz, Sheldon H. The State of Learning Disabilities: Facts, Trends and Emerging Issues. New York: National Center for Learning Disabilities, 2014. Retrieved from http://www.ncld.org/wp-content/uploads/2014/11/2014-State-of-LD.pdf

There are several types of learning disabilities. A language-based learning disability (**dyslexia**) that interferes with the ability to learn to read is the most common type of learning disability. Many professionals use the term "reading disability" to refer to all children on the continuum who have trouble with reading, ranging from mild to severe reading problems. Reading disabilities include those who are diagnosed with dyslexia. The term "reading disability" is used in this book to refer to all children who have difficulty with reading.

There are some common misconceptions about dyslexia. Many people think that individuals with dyslexia read backwards or see words as mirror images. This is not the case. While children with dyslexia will have difficulty reading, it is usually because they have trouble decoding, not because they "read backwards." Remember that reading is a very complex process that involves not one part of the brain, but many parts of the brain. *Anyone who proposes a simple explanation or simple solution to the problem is minimizing the demands of the task.*

Some people believe that dyslexia must be diagnosed by a medical doctor. Again, this is not the case. As discussed in the last chapter, dyslexia is diagnosed through a series of educational and psychological tests that are usually administered by a psychologist or learning disability specialist.

TYPES OF LEARNING DISABILITIES THAT AFFECT ACHIEVEMENT IN DIFFERENT AREAS[23]

▶ **Dysgraphia:** Difficulty with writing, which requires a complex set of motor and information processing skills.

▶ **Dyscalculia:** A math disability in which a student has difficulty with numbers and number concepts, learning math facts, and solving math problems.

▶ **Auditory processing disorders:** Difficulty understanding spoken language despite normal hearing.

▶ **Nonverbal learning disability (NVLD):** A learning disability that tends to progress with age. These children may be very verbal and decode well, but have trouble interpreting what they read. They often have trouble with socialization, making sense of information, putting together the parts to see the whole, and perceiving how things interact in physical space. Many individuals with NVLD develop problems with anxiety and depression.

▶ **Dyslexia:** A language-based learning disability that interferes with reading and other language-based skills, such as spelling and written language. This may also be referred to as a reading disability. It is the most common type of learning disability. Dyslexia is neurologically based and is not due to an impoverished environment or to poor instruction.

▶ **Reading disability:** A broad term used by many professionals that refers to all students who struggle with reading. This includes all those on the continuum who struggle with reading: from those with mild reading problems to those from the most severe end of the continuum, including those with dyslexia.

---

23   Cortiella, Candace and Horowitz, Sheldon H. The State of Learning Disabilities: Facts, Trends and Emerging Issues. New York: National Center for Learning Disabilities, 2014. Retrieved from http://www.ncld.org/wp-content/uploads/2014/11/2014-State-of-LD.pdf

WHO HAS TROUBLE LEARNING TO READ?

Reading problems exist in every public school in the country. It is estimated that between 38% and 40% of all students struggle with reading.[24] Clearly, not all of these children have dyslexia. Recall the continuum we just discussed. Most students require explicit and systematic phonics-based reading instruction. When this is available, most children will learn to read. When this is not available in the early grades, many may develop reading problems.

While difficulty learning to read affects children from all socio-economic, cultural, and racial backgrounds, certain groups are at greater risk for developing reading problems than others. At one time, educators believed that boys were

> **FACT:** Between 38% and 40% of all students struggle with reading.

more likely to experience reading problems than girls. While this is true, the ratio of boys to girls having reading problems is not as large as was once thought. Girls are less frequently identified as having reading problems because they are often less disruptive in the class-room and call less attention to themselves.

African American, Spanish-speaking, and American Indian students are much more likely to experience trouble learning to read.

> **FACT:** Both boys and girls may experience reading problems.

Approximately 53% of African American students, 52% of Hispanic students, and 48% of American Indian students experience reading problems.[25] The reasons for this are complex, but it is clear that poverty and the use of non-standard English and limited English proficiency play a role. Children

---

24 "Dr. G. Reid Lyon: Converging Evidence—Reading Research—What It Takes to Read," by Children of the Code, 2014. Retrieved from http://www.childrenofthecode.org/interviews/lyon.htm.
25 Ibid.

who live in poverty and who attend low-performing schools are more likely to have trouble learning to read.

WHY DO CHILDREN HAVE TROUBLE LEARNING TO READ?

Reading is one of the most important skills taught in school. It is the main focus of the educational curriculum in kindergarten and Grades 1, 2, and 3. If learning to read is such a priority for the child, the parent, and the school, why do so many children have trouble learning to read?

There are many reasons children experience difficulty learning to read. The landmark investigation into causes and prevention of reading problems by the National Research Council (1998)[26] identified three categories:

1. **Child risk factors:** Health and medical conditions linked to reading problems.

2. **Environmental risk factors:** Home environments that do not promote and support literacy skills are linked to reading problems.

3. **Educational risk factors:** Curriculum decisions made in the educational system that result in reading problems.

> **FACT:** The National Research Council cites genetic factors, environment, and poor-quality education as the major causes of reading problems.

---

26 *Preventing Reading Difficulties in Young Children,* by National Research Council (eds. C. Snow, M. S. Burns, and P. Griffin), 1998, Washington, DC: National Academy Press.

Child Risk Factors

Some children have a history of medical conditions, developmental delays, or genetic factors that predispose them to reading problems. Not all children with such histories will experience reading difficulty, but certain conditions are strongly related to difficulty learning to read.

- Children with a *family history of reading problems* are at greater risk for a reading disability. If a child's parents, siblings, grandparents, aunts, or uncles have a history of a reading disability, the child is more likely to develop a reading problem.

- Children with a *history of delayed language development* are at risk for reading problems. Research has shown that young children with early language impairment have a high incidence of subsequent reading problems.[27] The more persistent and severe the delay in language development, the more likely the child is to develop a reading problem. In my practice, I find that the majority of the children we see for reading concerns were slow in developing language skills. Their mothers frequently report that by the age of three, they could not be well understood by strangers.

- *Hearing impairment* or deafness is associated with reading difficulty. Chronic ear infections are often associated with intermittent hearing loss. These intermittent losses seem also to be associated with slow language development. More than half of the children I see in my practice have a history of chronic ear infections.

---

27   "Language Basis of Reading Disabilities and Implications for Early Identification and Remediation," by H. W. Catt and T. Hogan, 2003, *Special Education and Communication Disorders Faculty Publications,* 36, p. 234. Retrieved from http://digitalcommons.unl.edu/specedfacpub/36.

▶ *Attention-deficit disorder* contributes to trouble focusing and learning in the classroom in general, but *not to reading specifically.* However, there are many reasons why children are inattentive, and it is important to be cautious about accepting such a diagnosis. For example, anxiety can cause inattention. Children who have trouble processing language also become inattentive in the classroom because they have trouble following what is said. A diagnostician must rule out all competing possibilities for inattention before making a diagnosis of attention-deficit disorder. It is possible that your child actually has a reading disability but has been diagnosed with attention-deficit disorder. It is difficult to focus when you are unable to read the book that the other students are reading.

> **WARNING:** A diagnostician must rule out all competing possibilities for inattention before making a diagnosis of attention-deficit disorder.

Environmental Risk Factors

Reading is a language-based activity, and the language environment in a child's home is vitally important for early language development.

Children who come from a home environment that *does not promote and support literacy* are at risk for developing reading problems. It is critical for young children to interact verbally with adults in their environment and that adults read and talk with them on a regular basis. In some homes, children spend more hours in front of the TV screen or playing computer games than

> **FACT:** Young children need good language models and opportunities to practice verbal interactions on a regular basis.

they do interacting with their caretakers. Children need plenty of opportunities at home for verbal interaction with the adults in their world.

The 1998 National Research Council study of reading problems in the United States concluded that limited proficiency in English and the use of nonstandard English in the home can make it difficult for children to learn to read at school. Recall that reading is a language-based activity. When children are not proficient in English, or speak a dialect that differs phonologically in some ways from the mainstream English used in classrooms, they have difficulty distinguishing the sounds in English words. However, both Spanish and nonstandard dialects of English do overlap with mainstream English. Recent research outlines techniques teachers can use to teach linguistic minority students to read successfully.

Impoverished home environments and low-performing schools in poor neighborhoods and communities are often unable to provide the resources and support required for success in reading. Families in poverty are consumed by the need to survive and have difficulty finding time and money to devote to language-enriching activities. A parent who is desperately trying to keep the family safe, warm, and fed often does not have the means, time, or energy to do much else. Children growing up in poverty often enter kindergarten with much smaller vocabularies compared to children from middle-class and more affluent families. Early language development is extremely important—not only to reading but to all subsequent learning. When children come to school with low vocabularies, it is especially important for teachers to emphasize language activities.

> **FACT:** Children who live in poverty and who attend low-performing schools are more likely to have trouble learning to read.

You can help your child develop vocabulary and language skills by talking with them while at home, in the car, in the supermarket, at meal times, and while going about your daily activities. Talk to your children about the family, their toys, what you are preparing for dinner—anything that is going on in your life. Children love to play word games with adults, and you can play games in the car, while eating, or at any other time in the day.

Read to your child daily. With young children who are just learning to speak, start by just labeling pictures, by pointing to the pictures in the book and repeating the name of the item. As children get older you can begin to read age-appropriate picture books; make sure you talk about the pictures while you do this. When they are even older you can read age-appropriate chapter books. Discuss the books as you read them.

Educational Risk Factors

While child and family risk factors are considerable, a child's engagement with the educational system accounts for most reading problems; educational risk factors are the focus of this book.

Like Elena, some children learn to read regardless of the skill of the teacher or the reading method employed. You probably know some children who knew how to read before entering school. *However, for most kindergarten and first grade students, the training of the teacher and the methods used to teach reading are critical for success.* There are many students who would not have reading problems if they had been instructed appropriately in the early grades. These children are referred to by some professionals as "education casualties." While biological and background factors contribute to difficulty learning to read, the major contributor to reading problems is inadequate reading instruction in the early grades.

Most reading problems can be prevented with improved instruction in school. However, effective prevention requires strong educational leadership both from the universities who train our teachers and from public school administrators who oversee reading programs in the elementary schools.

Reading experts estimate that most *reading problems can be prevented* when teachers have the skills and knowledge to teach reading to all children who do not learn easily. It is necessary that schools provide appropriate instruction, with explicit and systematic phonics instruction in kindergarten and first, second, and third grade.[28] While some schools are excellent, there are simply not enough good schools, administrators, and

> **FACT:** Most reading problems can be prevented with explicit, systematic, phonics-based instruction in the early grades.

teachers. Many school systems *do not know how best to teach reading*. Their teachers and administrators are unfamiliar with the reading research and do not understand how to teach reading utilizing research-based instructional approaches.

Some schools have chronically low academic achievement among their students. It is very difficult for a student to receive an appropriate education in one of these substandard schools.

Many school systems *lack an integrated approach to teaching reading*. This means that instruction can vary from school to school in the same town. It also means that instruction can vary from teacher to teacher within the same school. Imagine the confusion this creates for struggling readers!

---

28   "The Prevention of Reading Difficulties," by J. Torgesen, 2002, *Journal of School Psychology*, Vol. 40(1), pp. 7-26. Retrieved from www.fcrr.org/publications/publicationspdffiles/prevention_reading.pdf.

It is common for a child to receive instruction in one method of reading in the first grade but to receive a different approach in the second grade. Many children actually receive *more than one method of reading instruction in the same year!* Often a struggling reader receives reading help from a special education teacher, a reading specialist, and the classroom teacher. These three teachers each use their own methodology for teaching reading and typically do not coordinate their instruction, often causing even more confusion for the student. This lack of coordination happens when leaders in the school system fail to enact policies that ensure an effective reading curriculum.

This all leads to the important question: What *does* work? How do you give your child every advantage in learning to read? How do you provide the solid foundation that will ward off problems so your child can use her reading skills to learn rather than continue to struggle throughout her reading career? As a parent, it is crucial that you know the answers to these questions as you advocate for your child.

CHAPTER SIX
WHAT WORKS

"Using evidence-based methods, it is possible to teach just about every child to read."[29]

—Sally E. Shaywitz, MD. and Bennett A. Shaywitz, MD
Authors of *"Armed With the Facts: The Science of Reading
and Its Implications for Teaching"*

Vanessa showed up in my office literally toting a large cardboard box. "I've just about had it!" she spouted. "First, I took my son to a tutoring chain that promised miracles. Next, I paid $400 for this program that my son's teacher assured me would work." She placed the box on a chair, pointing to a slick gold seal on the front. "I've even seen it on TV. But all it did for us was cause more headaches, more fights, and more frustration. It was just one more thing for me to try and get Brian to do. And at school, they had a tutor doing the same thing. None of it worked."

---

29   "Armed With the Facts: The Science of Reading and Its Implications for Teaching," by Sally E. Shaywitz, MD and Bennett A. Shaywitz, MD in *Why Kids Can't Read: Challenging the Status Quo in Education* (p. 19), edited by P. Blaunstein and R. Lyon, 2006, Lanham, MD: Rowman & Littlefield Education.

It is important that you, as a parent, are able to recognize the difference between appropriate reading instruction and inappropriate reading instruction. There is no mystery here. We know what works for the largest number of children. Decades of reading research make it clear.

Properly trained teachers who use methods based on research are able to teach nearly all of our children to read proficiently. Yes, even children and adults with severe reading disabilities can learn to read. However, inappropriate reading instruction in the early years, when children are first learning to read, can have significant negative consequences. In this

> **FACT:** Decades of reading research make it clear. We know what works to ensure that most children learn to read proficiently.

chapter, you will learn to recognize the elements of effective teaching for mainstream education in kindergarten through Grade 3 when children are first acquiring reading skills. You will also learn what works for remedial reading instruction for struggling readers who require extra help because they have fallen behind.

Understanding how to recognize the key elements of effective instruction for struggling readers is one of the most important steps you must take as a parent. It will help you make good educational decisions for your child. While similar teaching strategies are used for both beginning readers and struggling readers, there are additional issues to consider for children who have trouble reading and have fallen behind their classmates.

THE GREAT READING WARS

If you are reading this book because you have a struggling reader, it is likely that you are caught in the middle of the reading wars. The "great debate" of the past 60–70 years caused a serious divide in the field of reading. On the one side, "whole language" advocates called for an end to "drill and kill" worksheets and promoted an emphasis on teaching children to read by the sight-word method and providing exposure to literature. They argued that explicit phonics instruction was rarely, if ever, needed.

On the other side, proponents of phonics argued that children need systematic instruction in phonics in order to read, beginning with learning their letters and sounds. They maintained a strong emphasis on the need for explicit instruction with a phonics-based curriculum that went from easy to difficult in a systematic structured fashion.

Whole language: A teaching philosophy based on the belief that children discover how to read and spell on their own through an in-depth exposure to good literature.

Explicit, systematic phonics instruction (structured literacy): A teaching philosophy based on the belief that most children require direct, systematic teaching of phonics to become good readers.

As a result of the "whole language" movement, national reading scores plummeted. California became the prime example of the folly of this approach. In 1994, after that state mandated the use of whole language in all its public schools, their reading scores tied with Louisiana for dead last in the country. The debate over how best to teach reading has persisted in our country since the beginning of public education. The most recent battle has been particularly protracted and resulted in large numbers of children having reading problems.

Congress stepped in and declared reading, and the resultant low literacy problem, a national health concern and charged the National Institute of Child Health and Human Development (NICHD) with researching the issue. Researchers sought to understand the nature of the problem, why so many children have trouble learning to read, and how best to remedy the situation.

> **FACT:** NICHD has funded reading research for more than 40 years. The results of these studies have been published in thousands of professional journals and books.

EVIDENCE-BASED READING RESEARCH

In an attempt to end the "great reading debate" between phonics and whole language, researchers recognized the need to use scientifically based research methods. It would no longer do for developers of reading programs and publishing companies to conduct their own pseudo-research in an attempt to justify their own reading programs. Rigorous research methods needed to be used to determine which reading programs actually produced the best readers. Just as in medical research and new drug research, these studies needed to be well designed and carefully conducted by investigators with no stake in a specific reading method or in selling a particular reading series.

As you look at various research studies, it is important that you are able to recognize well-designed reading research. Rigorous, scientific studies include clear, well-documented details with a description of the setting in which the reading program was administered. This includes the characteristics of the children, the training of the teacher, the instructional method, and the population for whom the method was most effective. The highest-quality research studies are published in professional journals which require peer review and acceptance by professional experts before they can be published. This is a rigorous standard that is meant to determine which reading programs are effective for teaching the largest number of children.

Be aware that not every brightly pack-aged program that promises overnight results at home or school is backed by solid research. Even programs that claim to get results are often based on *anecdotal evidence*. This means that enthusiasm for the

> **FACT:** Research results have determined the important elements of effective reading instruction.

program is simply based on a few people who are willing to speak on behalf of the company.

The NICHD-funded research studied hundreds of thousands of children and adults from all parts of the country and from all backgrounds and ethnic groups. The results of these studies were summarized in a major national report by an independent panel of experts in reading and child development, the *National Reading Panel (NRP)*. This panel, supported by the NICHD but mandated by Congress, published their report in 2000. More recent studies have replicated and supported their results.[30]

The evidence from thousands of studies all led to the same conclusions. *Beginning readers learn best with structured, phonics-based programs. Many children will fall behind in reading without such a program.* While not all children need instruction in pho-nological awareness and

> **TIP:** The NRP **parent guide** describes early literacy activities to use with children at home and school to help them learn to read. The **teacher's guide** provides a framework for using the NRP findings in the classroom.

---

30   "National Reading Panel Publications," by National Institute of Child Health and Human Development, 2013. Retrieved from www.nichd.nih.gov/about/org/der/branches/cdbb/Pages/nationalreadingpanelpubs.aspx.

structured phonics, none are harmed by it. It is important for your child's kindergarten, first-, second-, and third-grade teachers to select evidence-based reading programs that will benefit the largest number of children. While some teachers may protest that not all students need direct phonics instruction, it is crucial to provide this solid base to ensure academic success for all children. *No child is harmed by phonics instruction, but many will be harmed by the absence of such instruction.* Jeanne Chall, a leader in the field of reading, was fond of comparing teaching phonics with a handicapped-accessible ramp. Not everyone can use steps, so if you have only one entryway, build the ramp.

Many professionals thought, given this conclusive body of evidence, the reading wars would finally come to an end. But it has not been that simple. Many educators feel strongly about how best to teach reading and have been reluctant to give up their old ways. Others simply do not possess the training and know-how to teach a sequential, systematic phonics program, especially if a child is not easily mastering reading. Many of our teachers today were taught to use whole language techniques in their teacher training programs and are not familiar with how to provide systematic phonics instruction. Such teaching requires some sophisticated knowledge of the English language and its sound and spelling systems. Despite all of the research, few colleges of education provide this training. Some teachers learn this later as part of their continuing education, but too many do not have this expertise.

> **FACT:** Research shows that structured, phonics-based instruction for beginning readers ensures that the largest number of children will learn to read.

LEARN HOW YOUR CHILD IS BEING TAUGHT

1. **Ask** your child's teacher in grades K–3 questions about the curriculum she uses. You want to know if she is using a structured phonics program and what *training* she has had in the use of that curriculum as well as in reading in general. Keep asking until you understand. Remember, if you don't understand the answer, perhaps the person doing the explaining is not clear about it either.

2. **Monitor** your child's work papers as they come home. Have your child *read them out loud to you*. You can learn a lot about the reading instruction taking place in the classroom by going over these papers. By having children read assignments orally, you can see if they are able to do the work and if they are learning to sound out words. If no papers come home, ask the teacher to show you his work.

3. **Talk** to your child. Ask questions about what is happening in school. What is he reading in school? Does he like it? What is it about? Who does he read with in class? When do they have reading during the day? How much time do they spend reading during the day? Do they use workbooks? You know the drill. Children are not always forthcoming about their day. But you've been doing this for years. Keep asking.

If your school system is not using a structured phonics approach, there are very likely many students in your community who are having trouble learning to read. You are not alone.

WHAT WORKS FOR BEGINNING READERS

If your child is struggling with reading, then the reading instruction is not working for him. It's that simple. In order to understand why your child's reading instruction program is not working, it is important to know the different components of a good reading program. There are a series of steps each child must master in order to learn to read. The progression from one step to the next step is important for successful reading development.

Research studies yield consistent results and highlight the same themes over and over again. The different elements of effective reading instruction must include:

> **TIP:** An effective reading program includes instruction in phonological awareness, phonics, fluency, vocabulary, and reading comprehension.

- ▸ Phonological awareness instruction

- ▸ Systematic and direct phonics instruction, which must also include teaching children nonphonetic sight words

- ▸ Teaching to mastery

- ▸ Training in oral reading fluency

- ▸ Instruction in vocabulary

- ▸ Instruction in reading comprehension

Let's look at what these terms mean and how you can recognize them. You can determine whether each of these is being taught to your child even if you are not trained in these methods.

Phonological Awareness Instruction

As we have discussed, phonological awareness instruction means teaching children that the words they hear spoken can be broken into parts. They learn that spoken words have individual sounds. Most children, if taught well, master phonological awareness in kindergarten.

They learn about rhyming and how to identify the beginning and ending sounds in words.

For example, they come to recognize that

► the word *cat* has three sounds: /c/-/a/-/t/

► *cat* rhymes with *mat, sat,* and *hat*

► *cat* has the same beginning sound as *kiss, car,* and *candy*

► *cat* has the same ending sound as *hit, pet,* and *chat*

► each sound in *cat* is represented by a letter

► in a stage we call **alphabetics**, children learn to associate sounds with letters and learn the names of the letters

This instruction should begin in kindergarten. Ask your child's teacher how she is providing phonological awareness instruction and what curriculum she is using.

> **TIP:** Examples of phonological tasks can be seen on the kindergarten screening video at www.SmartKidCantRead.com.

Children who have weak phonological skills are at risk for having difficulty learning to read. This is a critical foundational skill. If you have questions about your child's phonological skills, you can begin by administering the kindergarten tests found in Appendix A or at *www.SmartKidCantRead*.com. This is an informal test that parents can administer to their own children and will give you an idea if your concerns are justified. If you find that your child is having a little trouble in this area, there are many things that you can do at home to help your child at this early stage in his or her development.

PARENT ACTIVITIES FOR PHONOLOGICAL AWARENESS

▶ Read books with your child daily. There are many wonderful children's books that play with sounds and rhyming and focus on letter sounds. The Dr. Seuss books, the Mother Goose rhymes, and the Letterland Alphabet books are three good examples.

▶ Play word games. Children love playing word games with adults. Take turns thinking of animals that begin with the /m/ sound, or foods that begin with the /b/ sound . . . make up your own.

▶ Take turns thinking of a word that begins with the last sound of the previous word: If I say snake, the last sound in snake is /k/, so your word must begin with the /k/ sound.

▶ Try a variation of "I Spy." Identify an object in the room for your child to guess. I spy something that begins with the /t/ sound.

▶ Put it to music. Singing and clapping engage the rhythm and sounds of words.

▶ Print out professional materials. You can find many activities at www.fcrr.org. While these are designed for teachers, many can be used in the home.

Six to eight weeks of help in the summer can go a long way at this stage of a child's reading development. If your child is having trouble, find a tutor to work on phonological skills, identification of letters, the sounds of letters, and writing letters. Begin blending sounds into words. A good tutor will understand that instruction in phonological awareness should overlap with beginning instruction in phonics. I recommend tutoring for a *minimum* of two to three times per week because any less than that does not provide enough continuity—children need repetition to help consolidate what they are learning, and they need practice to help them master new skills. Reinforce the new learning between tutoring sessions by working at home (15–20 minutes per day) with assignments the tutor can provide. Keep it fun. Children at this age are eager to learn to read and have not yet encountered the frustrations of failure.

Remember, you want a tutor with expertise in reading and with experience in helping struggling readers. You are looking for someone who is trained and experienced in one of the structured phonics-based reading programs or in one of the multisensory structured language reading approaches. Ask her if she is certified in the use of the program. Speak to other parents about their experience with the tutor. You want your child tutored 2–5 times per week, depending on the age of your child and the severity of his problem. Younger children or those with less severe problems need 2–3 times per week. Older children or those with more severe reading problems need 4–5 times per week. You can now make an informed choice when choosing a tutor for your child.

Systematic and Explicit Phonics Instruction (Structured Literacy)

With phonics, children learn the relationship between sounds and letters. There is a well-established sequence of phonics instruction that goes from easy to more difficult. This is called **systematic phonics instruction**. Such teaching must be **cumulative**; it is important that students have appropriately sequenced instruction that builds skills in a logical

> **Multisensory structured language reading approaches** (structured literacy) use sequential phonics instruction with auditory, visual, and kinesthetic techniques to enhance learning.

order, beginning with the simplest phonics rules and progressing to the more complex principles.

Instruction typically begins by teaching children the sounds of the consonants and short vowels and then showing them how to blend those sounds into simple words with a beginning consonant, one vowel, and an ending consonant. For example:

m-a-t

p-i-n

h-o-p

t-e-n

After this has been mastered, children are typically taught words that contain consonant digraphs, such as -ch, -sh, and -th. **A consonant digraph** is *two* consonants that are grouped together to make *one* sound, such as in:

*sh*op

*ch*ip

wi*th*

*wh*en

Children may next be taught how to blend words containing consonant blends, such as br-, tr-, and -st. **Consonant blends** are two or more consonants grouped together, in which each consonant makes a *separate* sound, thus producing two or more distinct sounds, such as in:

*br*ag

*tr*im

li*st*

strip

This may be followed by lessons on the effects of the final silent "e." **Silent e rule:** In a one syllable word, when there is a vowel followed by a consonant and an *e* at the end of the word, the final *e* is silent and the vowel makes a long sound. Examples include:

m*ate*

p*ine*

h*ope*

m*u*le

This sequential phonics instruction should be the focus of the reading curriculum in the first and second grades and should continue until a child has acquired the basic skills of how to sound out words. *While there are variations in the sequence of phonetic skills taught, the point is that there **is** a sequence.* Some programs provide phonics instruction in a haphazard, nonsequential manner and teach children how to sound out only when they encounter words they can't read. They call this "embedded phonics." This type of instruction is problematic for a child who is experiencing any confusion with reading.

Skills that are directly taught by the teacher are called **explicit instruction**. Explicit phonics instruction does not involve guessing based on the pictures, or asking children what they think a word should say based on the content of what they are reading. While such strategies may come later, they should not be the basis of instruction. Good, clear instruction explains and demonstrates to children how to blend sounds together to form words and how to sound out words, and then helps them practice these skills. Remember, reading is not a natural activity, like walking or speaking.

ACT: Systematic and explicit phonics instruction should be the main focus of the curriculum in kindergarten and Grades 1, 2, and 3 in all schools. Ask your child's teacher what reading program or method she uses.

Our brains are not hardwired to know how to read. We need to learn how to "crack the code." While proponents of whole language may speak disparagingly about such practices as "drill and kill," phonics activities can be fun. You can make it fun at home, and teachers can make it fun in the classroom. Most children love to learn.

Instruction in Sight Words

While phonics instruction is important, children also need to learn some words by sight since some of our most frequently used words cannot be read phonetically. For example, commonly used words such as *some, as, come, are, two, does, the, here, of,* and *one* cannot be sounded out or read phonetically.

Teach to Mastery

Reading is a *cumulative* process that builds on prior skills. *Teaching to mastery means children must be able to read on one level before moving on to the next.* This is an important concept because reading builds on skills previously taught. Children who have not mastered skills at the beginning level before moving on to a more challenging level will have problems. For

> **TIP:** Children need to master one reading level before moving on to the next level.

example, children who have not learned the letters of the alphabet and the sounds of each letter will have trouble when the teacher introduces more difficult phonics skills, such as consonant blends and two syllable words. Children must master the basic concepts of phonics if they are to become good readers. *Put simply, you cannot skip the basics. Children must be taught at their own level of instruction.* Children cannot learn when teaching is not at their skill level. They become overwhelmed. This leads to frustration and falling further behind. Imagine trying to take the third year of Spanish before taking Spanish 1 and 2. This is exactly the level of frustration many children experience in school on a daily basis. If your child is struggling with reading and the teacher is not providing ample time and opportunity for him to master one reading level before going on to the next, you need to get help!

Children learn to read at different rates. Some learn quickly and become proficient readers by the end of the first grade. Others will need more time to learn and master the phonics concepts. However, a classroom teacher *cannot, and does not*, teach each child in the classroom a separate lesson designed just for him! The only way for a teacher to realistically accommodate these different rates of learning is to have reading groups that function at different levels.

Some schools fear that grouping stigmatizes students. However, it has been my observation that children frequently prefer grouping. Children who need more instructional time feel less embarrassed when they are with others who have the same skill level. They are less worried about making mistakes and do not experience the loss of

During my first year as a fifth grade teacher, I had an interesting experience with grouping. I taught in a building that had three fifth grades. We divided all the fifth graders into ability groups for reading and math. As the new teacher, I was assigned the lowest group for math. I knew many of the children in my math group from my homeroom, where they seldom volunteered to speak in class. I watched them blossom in this math group; they felt free to speak up and take risks. We all had a wonderful time and, as a group, they did extremely well. Several of the children outperformed students in the math group above them. If these students had not been grouped, they would likely have remained reserved and less willing to take chances . . . and been less successful in math.

self-esteem that comes from feeling that they will never be as good as the child who is learning to read with ease. However, when I visit classrooms, I frequently see teachers who are trying to teach reading to a whole class of 25+ students. While some instruction can be given to the whole group, additional teaching must be provided in small groups in order for children to work at their own level until they have achieved mastery and to receive individual attention when needed. If your child is in a reading group, check to see if the teacher monitors progress so that children can change groups as they develop mastery.

Fluency Training

Fluency refers to the ability to read words and passages automatically and at a good rate of speed. If you ask your child to read out loud for you, it will become obvious if he is having difficulty reading automatically and with fluency. His reading will be slow and labored—a painful experience. Difficulty reading fluently is usually related to trouble with decoding. The child who cannot automatically sound out words struggles and reads at a slow rate. Some children are slow at taking in all types of information, while others are slow with language-related issues, such as listening, reading, and writing. All of these can result in fluency problems.

Often the best remedy for problems with fluency is to practice reading the same passages two or three times. Begin by having your child read the passage silently. Next, he can follow along while you read aloud. Then, read the passage aloud together. Finally, he can read it orally by himself. There are several

> **Fluency** refers to the ability to read words and passages automatically and at an appropriate rate of speed.

fluency programs that provide opportunity for repeated reading. Students read each passage several times until they have achieved a designated level of speed and then go on to the next, slightly more difficult passage. This is a skill that can be practiced at home as well as in school.

If your child is receiving help in reading fluency, the level of the reading passages should be coordinated with the level of phonics instruction. For example, it doesn't make sense for a child to receive fluency instruction at a fifth grade level and instruction in phonics at a second grade level. *Passages for practicing fluency should be at a level slightly lower than a child's instructional level in phonics so he is practicing material that he has already been taught and mastered.*

> **TIP:** *Read Naturally* and *Great Leaps* are two fluency programs that provide passages for repeated readings. Great Leaps has a home version you can download at www.greatleaps.com.

It is important to note that when a child is laboring to read, instruction should focus on the underlying cause—his weak decoding ability. Fluency training should be coordinated within the context of a complete, structured phonics program.

Instruction in Vocabulary and Reading Comprehension

Most children who struggle with reading have difficulty with decoding, or sounding out words. While fewer struggling readers have trouble with reading comprehension, this is still an important area. The whole point of reading is to derive meaning from what we read.

Reading comprehension is related to the ability to understand what we hear (our receptive oral language ability). It should be taught by discussing stories and with explicit instruction in vocabulary, sentence structure, and paragraph formation. Most elementary school teachers are good at discussing fictional stories with the class. I seldom see this level of attention paid to nonfiction, which requires different comprehension strategies. The new Common Core focus on informational text emerged from the finding that today's students do not receive enough instruction in interpreting and analyzing nonfiction text. This puts them at a disadvantage when they enter high school and college and have trouble understanding their textbooks. Even in the upper elementary and middle school grades, we expect children to learn through their reading, and most of what we ask them to read is not literature but informational text.

Vocabulary development is crucial for students who have trouble with reading comprehension. In fact, *all* children need continuing work on learning new and increasingly difficult words. We all encounter new vocabulary throughout our entire lives. Students in school need to learn the meanings of word parts, such as prefixes and suffixes, and understand how to combine them to create new words, as in: *engage, disengage, re-engage, engagement, engaging,* and *engaged.* Most children are acquainted with the normal range of vocabulary we use when we speak. However, they often need explicit instruction in vocabulary that appears in higher-level reading texts or even the academic vocabulary that teachers use in giving them instructions in class.

> **Reading comprehension** is the ability to understand what is read. Children who struggle with reading comprehension require a different type of remediation than children who struggle with decoding.

To enhance reading comprehension, it is also important to teach students sentence structure by, once again, going from simple to complex. Instruction begins with simple sentences, adding phrases and clauses, and finally combining simple sentences to form compound and complex sentences. Similarly, paragraph instruction proceeds from simple to complex as children learn to identify topic and ending sentences and the main points of paragraphs. They then learn to write different types of paragraphs, such as comparison and cause-and-effect paragraphs. All of these elements (vocabulary development, sentence structure, and paragraphing) are part of a good program in reading comprehension.

These same elements (vocabulary development, sentence structure, and paragraphing) provide the backbone for effective instruction in written lan-

> **TIP:** Remediation in reading comprehension should include instruction in vocabulary development, sentence structure, and paragraphing.

guage. *Reading comprehension and written language are complementary processes. When you work on one area, you strengthen the other.* As students learn to *write* sentences and paragraphs with increasing linguistic complexity, they also learn to derive meaning as they *read* more complex text.

While children are catching up with their decoding skills and cannot read independently at grade level, it is a good idea for parents to read their classroom textbooks and assignments aloud

> **TIP:** As students learn to write sentences and paragraphs with increasing complexity, they also learn to derive meaning as they read more complex text.

to them. This exposes them to higher-level vocabulary and sentence structure and allows them to access the information other students get by reading.

A Fully Coordinated Program

Many of you will be told, when you ask, that your child's teacher does not use one specific reading curriculum. The principal or teachers may say, "Our school does not believe in using only one program." They may state that no single method will work for all children. Perhaps the school has developed their own approach or pulled from several different programs. There may also be a political side to the decision not to have a system-wide reading curriculum. Many school systems do not want to tell teachers how to teach. They do not want to interfere with the teacher's right to make decisions in her own classroom.

There are several problems with this approach. While it is true that no one program is right for every student, very few teachers or schools possess the expertise required to put together a solid, success-

> **TIP:** Schools need an evidence-based reading curriculum that is coordinated across the district.

ful reading curriculum that spans the needs of children with widely divergent skills. Doing so requires an intimate knowledge of the relationship between language and reading and a deep understanding of the language skills that children must possess to learn to read. Creating a successful reading program also requires an expert's knowledge of the structure of phonics and how to best present phonics principles to children. I have observed hundreds of teachers over the years, but I have encountered only a handful who were capable of successfully teaching reading without the use of an evidenced-based reading program or training in an evidence-based method of instruction. If teachers are skilled at teaching using a comprehensive, research-based program of reading instruction, they will also be more likely to know how to adapt certain aspects of that program for individual students who are struggling!

A good school-wide reading curriculum for beginning readers helps teachers structure learning and outlines an appropriate sequence of instruction, providing continuity from one grade to another and among teachers of the same grade. Teachers often talk to me about the lack of continuity of reading instruction in their building. *"Every year, I have to catch up half my class,"* one teacher confided in me. *"Those who come from the room beside me are fine. But the children two doors down... Now that's a different story. I have to spend the first half of the year trying to get those children caught up!"* I'm sure you know which teachers in your child's school are preferable to others. This parent "hotline" of information has become such an issue with school systems that most systems refuse to accept parent requests for student placement with specific teachers.

Many school systems announce that they use a **"balanced approach."** If this is what you are told, ask for specific information about the school's phonics instruction. A balanced approach often means that the school is still using the *whole language* method with little or no explicit, sequential phonics instruction. While "balanced" sounds good, the balance often is lacking. If taught at all, phonics is incidental or "embedded" and taught only "as needed." Such programs lack the explicit, systematic, and sequential teaching that is so crucial to effective reading instruction. This generally ad hoc method of teaching disadvantages the many children who need the systematic approach.

WHAT WORKS FOR STRUGGLING READERS

Children who have trouble learning in the mainstream classroom often receive special help in reading. However, *inappropriate* remedial reading instruction for children who have already fallen behind can result in a loss of self-esteem, wasted valuable time, and falling yet further behind their classmates. Many begin to feel hopeless when they receive extra help in reading that doesn't make a difference. "I will *never* learn to read. I just don't care." They may lose trust that anyone can help them.

We must look at our failure through their eyes. A child who receives extra help but continues to struggle with reading despite that help believes *he* is the problem. Such children begin to think of themselves as stupid. They do not question their teachers. They do not recognize that *how* they are being instructed is at fault. When we provide students with the wrong type of reading help and they do not make progress, they begin to think of themselves as inferior and unteachable.

Help for the struggling reader can take many forms, depending upon your community and resources available. Some children will receive **Title I** reading help. Others will work with **reading specialists**. Some will receive **special education** services, and others will be placed in **response to intervention (RTI)** classrooms. Many children will receive **private tutoring** after school. Some children will receive help in more than one program at the same time.

Response to intervention (RTI): A tiered program in which Tier 1 is the mainstream classroom education, Tier 2 provides specialized instruction for struggling readers, and higher tiers provide more intensive, specialized instruction for readers having trouble.

Title I programs: Federally funded programs provided to schools in economically designated areas for help in reading and math.

Special education programs: Instruction provided by special education teachers. Special education programs must follow the regulations in IDEA 2004.

Evidence-Based Principles of Instruction for Struggling Readers

The same principles of instruction that we discussed for beginning readers apply to struggling readers, regardless of where they receive their instruction. Elements of the program should include instruction in the following areas:

- ▸ Phonological awareness

- ▸ Explicit instruction in structured phonics and sight words

- ▸ Fluency training

- ▸ Vocabulary instruction

- ▸ Reading comprehension

- ▸ Teaching to mastery

However, the stakes are much higher for students who have fallen behind in reading because it is necessary not only to learn to read but to do so at a rate that is *more rapid* than their peers if they are to close their reading gap. Children who have fallen behind their classmates in learning to read require intensive remediation with a reading specialist who is trained and experienced in evidence-based reading instruction. An individual evaluation will highlight the areas that require remediation. Jerome provides a good example here.

Jerome was in the fifth grade when we first met. His parents noticed his difficulty learning to read by the middle of his first grade year. They spoke with his first-grade teacher, who was very kind and caring. She assured them there were several children in her class who were at the same level as Jerome. There was no need to be concerned; he would learn when he was ready. Besides, boys were often slower than girls to catch on to reading. She assured them that all children eventually learned to read. His parents accepted this.

But Jerome didn't learn to read in the second grade, despite being placed midyear in a Title I reading group for extra help. His parents did not know what type of reading instruction he received in that group. By the time Jerome was in the third grade, he disliked school and hated reading. Midway through the third grade, he was placed in a response to intervention (RTI) reading program in his classroom. Again, his parents did not know to ask what reading curriculum was being used. He was referred for a special education evaluation by his teacher in the fourth grade. As a result of this referral, he was tested and was determined to have a "specific learning disability," and special education reading services were initiated.

He received help from the special education teacher twice per week in a small group of six children. Although his reading teacher said he was making excellent progress, his parents could not see any difference. Jerome still could not read his homework assignments or manage any of his work independently. He was getting in trouble in school and not paying attention in class. His teachers thought his lack of motivation and attentional issues were the problem. When his parents asked whether he was dyslexic, they were told that was an old-fashioned term never used any more. As you can see, Jerome's parents had their concerns all along but did not act on them. They did not know how to ask for information about what was actually being done to help Jerome. They did not know what to look for.

When I saw Jerome as a **fifth grade** student, my testing revealed that he was a boy of high-average intelligence who was reading at a mid-second-grade level. My observation of his special education reading group revealed that these six students were each at different skill levels but instruction was all at the same level. Furthermore, the teacher was teaching at a level well above Jerome's reading ability, and he could not keep up with the others.

Small-group instruction—especially when the group members were all at different levels of reading—simply could not provide him with the individualization that he required in order to learn to read. While his teacher was using the Wilson Reading System, an effective, multisensory, structured language reading method designed for struggling readers, she was not certified in the use of the program and did not understand how to use it. Furthermore, reading help twice a week for half an hour for a student who is 3 years below grade level is just not enough. Not only is twice per week insufficient, but 30-minute sessions for a group of six is simply not long enough. Bear in mind that it takes a group of six students about 5–10 minutes to transition to the separate room and settle down to work. **There were only 16 minutes of actual instruction time the day of my observation—for six students!**

My evaluation revealed that Jerome had not made progress since the beginning of his special education reading help a year ago. In fact, the **reading gap** between his performance and that of his peers had actually continued to widen since he had begun to receive help in special education. His school had not monitored his progress in a manner that would provide this information for his parents.

What did Jerome need? He needed a program that could provide **structured phonics instruction along with fluency training**. *While his teacher's choice of the Wilson Reading System was an appropriate choice, he needed a teacher who was* **experienced** *and* **certified** *in the use of this program. Jerome needed* **1:1 instruction every day for 45–60 minutes per day**. *He did not appear to have difficulty with reading comprehension; in fact, he frequently tried to salvage himself by guessing at words based on the content of what he could deduce from his reading. However, in a case like Jerome's, it is always important to continue to monitor comprehension as students advance from one level of decoding to the next and the reading becomes more difficult.*

Jerome also needed **coordination** *of his reading remediation with his classroom work. For example, we decided to have his reading teacher individualize his classroom weekly spelling list so that she provided him with words that were consistent with the phonics principles they were working on in his reading tutorial.*

He additionally required some **accommodations** *while he was working to catch up with his peers. We decided to provide him with audio books for social studies and science because he could not read his books independently. Test questions were read to him, and he was given extended time to complete tests and some assignments.*

Once we solidified Jerome's program at school, it was important that he not lose momentum over the summer. However, the school told his parents they were not required by law to teach anything new during the summer or for Jerome to make academic progress during the summer months. They were required only to provide instruction to "prevent regression of skills." The school maintained that Jerome had never shown regression during the summer. In fact, his skills were too low to be able to determine whether he had actually regressed. As we persisted, the school system agreed to group instruction twice per week for 6 weeks. His parents wisely decided not to accept the group instruction and, instead, provided him with private, one-to-one tutoring four times a week throughout the summer. They felt they could not afford to lose those valuable summer months when Jerome could make progress without the added pressure of trying to keep up with other subjects. Their goal was to have their son reading at grade level by the time he entered middle school in 2 years. No more time could be wasted.

Like Jerome, *most children who have trouble learning to read have difficulty with phonological awareness and decoding.* That is, they struggle to sound out words and cannot read words automatically. It is essential that their remediation begin by first determining their reading level and the level at which they first encountered difficulty. That is the level at which their instruction must begin if they are to become proficient readers. This may mean that, for example, a fifth grade student must begin instruction at the beginning level of reading if that is his instructional level. *You just can't skip the basics.*

> **FACT:** Children who have difficulty learning to read require intensive remediation in an evidence-based method of instruction with a trained and experienced teacher.

Multisensory Structured Language Reading Approaches (Structured Literacy)

Now that you know the elements of a good evidence-based reading program, it is time to consider some of the programs that incorporate those principles.

In the 1930s, Samuel Torrey Orton and Anna Gillingham developed an intensive, phonics-based reading approach that taught children through multisensory pathways using visual, auditory, and kinesthetic techniques. They used diagnostic teaching methods to individualize instruction for children. Over the years, several other multisensory structured language reading methods have developed as derivatives of the Orton Gillingham approach. The International Dyslexia Association cites the following programs:

- ► Alphabetic Phonics

- ► Association Method

- ► Language!

- ► Lexia-Herman Method

- ► Lindamood-Bell

- ► Project Read

- ► The Slingerland Approach

- ► Sonday System

- ► Sounds In Syllables

- ► Spalding Method

- ► Starting Over

- ► Wilson Reading System

These methods all require specific teacher training and have been used successfully in schools that specialize in working with dyslexic students. If one of these programs is being used, make sure your teacher has been *certified* in the use of the program. As Jerome's parents learned, this is a critical issue. They were told that their son's teacher was "trained" in the program, but in fact she had only attended an introductory overview. She had not completed the year-long "certification" training program and therefore was unable to effectively teach the program as it was designed. Unfortunately, rather than understand the importance of expert and efficient instruction with a student who was significantly delayed in reading, the director of special education stated they were not required (by law) to train teachers in specific reading programs.

As we have seen in the case of Jerome, there are several issues unique to children who receive special help in reading.

SPECIAL CONSIDERATIONS FOR STRUGGLING READERS

- ▶ **Evidence-based reading approaches.** You want a reading program with a proven track record of helping struggling readers. In most cases, you cannot afford to go with a teacher-made program at this point. There are only a select few reading specialists with advanced degrees in reading or learning disabilities who possess expertise in helping struggling readers without the use of a specific method.

- ▶ **Teacher certification.** You want a reading teacher who is *trained and certified* in the use of the reading program or method she is teaching. Most multisensory structured language reading methods designed for remediation of the struggling reader require extensive teacher training. Unfortunately, this is not something that can be taken for granted. *It is important that you check on* *the teacher's training in the reading remediation program she is using.* In my professional experience, I often hear that parents have been told that a teacher is trained—only to discover later that this is not accurate. In some cases, the teacher only took an introductory seminar and did not complete the training that would teach her how to effectively implement the program. Checking this out is not difficult. Simply contact the facility where the teacher received her training. Most programs maintain lists of everyone who has completed their training. While schools are not required by law to train teachers in specific reading programs, most, unlike Jerome's school, acknowledge the need for certification training in order to effectively teach when they use one of these programs.

▸ **Coordination** of all language arts instruction is important for success. This means remedial reading services need to be coordinated with classroom instruction in reading, spelling, and written language. If a child is receiving speech and language therapy, that should also be part of this coordination. If there is more than one type of reading instruction taking place with more than one teacher, you need to question why this is happening. Can this be streamlined and taught by one teacher? *It is not uncommon for a child to have reading instruction with two or three different reading teachers who never coordinate with one another.* A child might be learning to read the words *station, invention,* and *combination* with one teacher, while working on words like *stop, club, lock,* and *brick* with another. These word groups represent two very different levels of skill development. This just confuses a child and interferes with learning to mastery.

*Always remember to include teacher coordination time in your child's **individualized education program (IEP)** to ensure that it takes place.* You cannot assume this will actually happen unless it is written into the IEP. If you have a private reading tutor in addition to the reading services at school, remember that the same principles of instruction apply. Coordination with the private tutor should also be included in the IEP.

▸ **Accommodations.** The student who is several years below grade level in reading and unable to manage his classwork or homework independently will require accommodations while he is receiving intensive remediation. Accommodations make it possible for children to make progress in subjects such as science and social studies. For example, your child might be provided with material to read for science class that is written on a lower grade level than his textbook. However, *do not ever allow accommodations to take the place of teaching your child to read.*

I have sat in many team meetings and heard school personnel tell parents they do not need to worry about how well their child reads. As long as he is able to understand the content of the curriculum in the various subjects, he will be fine. Besides, there just isn't enough time in his schedule to offer the amount of reading help he needs. They explain to parents the accommodations they can offer, such as text-to-speech programs, audio books, scribes, readers for tests, and more. These can be helpful accommodations, but don't let them take the place of appropriate reading instruction. Schools must teach children to read!

> **WARNING:** Do not allow accommodations to take the place of teaching your child to read.

▶ **Frequency** of remediation. There is a basic rule of thumb that can be helpful in guiding you when making decisions about how often your child needs extra reading help. *The more severe the reading disability, the more frequently your child needs to be seen.* A child with a mild reading disability who may be only 1 year below grade level requires less help than a child who has a severe reading disability and is 2 or more years below grade level. For a child with a reading disability serious enough to qualify him for special education help, I would recommend a *minimum of three times per week.* For a child with a severe disability, I would recommend *five* times per week.

Don't overlook the summer. Summer is an important time to provide students with remediation because they do not have the pressure of trying to keep up with their subjects at the same time. If your school insists on providing only minimal services to prevent "regression of skills," think about opting for private tutoring if you can.

▶ **Grouping** of students who require special reading help outside of the mainstream classroom is another issue that depends on the severity of the reading disability. Children with severe reading disabilities require *individual* help. If your school is recommending grouping, there are several points to consider:

- All children in the reading group should be at the same reading level with similar needs. Just because they are in the same grade does not mean they are at the same level. (Schools can provide you with information about the reading levels of the other students without compromising the confidentiality of the children.)

- Research has shown that groups of two to three students tend to work best. At this size, a good teacher can still provide individualization when your child needs it. Based on my own experience and observations, I do not recommend larger groups.

- More time needs to be allocated when children are grouped together. Jerome's half-hour session for a group of six children was just not long enough. You

> **TIP:** The choice of reading program, teacher expertise, coordination of services, use of accommodations, frequency of remediation, grouping, and monitoring of progress are critical to your child's remediation success.

need a full hour-long period, keeping in mind that a 1-hour period does not translate to an hour of actual instruction time.

- Grouping, when done well, can be beneficial. Sessions can be enjoyable and stimulating for children. On the other hand, when students are not well matched in terms of reading ability and personality, grouping becomes a lost opportunity.

▶ **Monitoring reading progress** is an essential part of the remediation process. You need to know if the remediation is working and if your child is making appropriate progress. *What is appropriate progress?* If you want your child to catch up and learn to read at grade level, this means he will need to make *more than 1 year's progress* in an academic year. Your school may tell you this is unrealistic and cannot be done. *It can be done, and*

> **TIP:** Children who are below grade level in reading must make more than 1 year's progress for every year in school if they are to close the gap between their reading skills and the skills of their peers.

—— 139 ——

is done, by good, well-trained reading teachers. I strongly recommend that you work with an independent evaluator you trust to have this evaluation completed at the end of each academic year. Remember, when monitoring annual educational progress, use standardized tests and compare standard scores and percentile ranks as described in Chapter 4.

In addition to monitoring reading progress at the end of the school year with standardized tests, the teacher should be completing informal progress monitoring throughout the year to determine whether the reading instruction is working. This informal progress monitoring is important so teachers can adjust their instruction to meet the needs of your child as he makes progress or to change the instruction if it is not effective.

In an effective multisensory structured language-based program, you may see your child demonstrate progress in reading nonsense words before they show growth in any of the other areas. They are not likely to show significant progress in word list reading or passage reading at the beginning stage while they are working to build a solid foundation using phonetically regular words.

▶ **Classroom observation.** It is always important to monitor what is actually going on in the classroom. Make sure there is a fit between what you are being told and what is actually being taught. You must make sure that your school is not just paying lip service to appropriate reading instruction. Your evaluator can do classroom observations for you or you can do them yourself. Visit the classroom during your child's language arts/reading instruction. If he receives reading instruction in another setting as well as the classroom, make sure you observe in *all* settings where he receives reading instruction. You want to observe how he is doing, the materials being used, and how he is managing the curriculum. Find out if the instruction in the different settings is coordinated. Ask to see his work folders. If you are uncomfortable making an appointment to do an observation, offer to volunteer in your child's classroom during the period when they have reading instruction. This will give you an opportunity to see what is going on.

HOW TO SELECT A TUTOR

▶ Referral. Contact organizations such as the *International Dyslexia Association* or the *Learning Disabilities Association* for references of tutors in your area. Speak to other parents for referrals of tutors who have been helpful. Contact training programs that specialize in multisensory structured reading approaches, such as *The Orton Gillingham Academy, The Academic Language Therapists Association,* and *Wilson Language Training* for a list of certified tutors in your area.

▶ Training. Look for a tutor who is certified in one of the multisensory structured language reading approaches recommended for struggling readers.

▶ Experience. Select a tutor who is certified in the use of a remedial reading program and who is experienced. An experienced tutor will know how to coordinate with classroom teachers and classroom instruction. Experienced tutors will know how to handle issues of attention and motivation.

▶ Location. Where will the tutoring take place? Can the tutor come into the school to tutor during reading time in a private office? Will the tutoring take place in your home, in the tutor's office, or in the local library?

▶ Timing. An experienced tutor will understand that a first or second grader may be tired after school and not have much energy for tutoring. Is there time before school? Is there time for one of the sessions on a weekend? Can your child go into school an hour late so he can receive tutoring in the morning? Can the tutor go into the school?

▶ Frequency. How often will your child be tutored? Less than twice per week does not provide enough continuity to make meaningful progress. Children with severe reading problems or who are significantly delayed in their reading should be seen 4–5 times per week.

▶ Length of session. Most tutoring sessions are 45–60 minutes in length. If your child is in kindergarten or first grade, you may start with 30 minutes and build up to 45–60-minute sessions. Remember this rule of thumb: Children with severe reading problems and those who are significantly delayed in their reading skills require reading help on a more frequent basis and will require a longer period of time to close the gap between their skills and the skills of their peers. Even children with severe reading disabilities can learn to read.

You now have an idea of the educational issues and what to request for reading instruction for beginning and struggling readers. In some systems, it will be a joy to work collaboratively with staff on behalf of your child. Other systems are more resistant to parent requests that differ from their recommendations. If you find yourself in that situation, you will need to learn something about your rights under the *Individuals with Disabilities in Education Act (IDEA)* 2004. The next chapter will provide you with some of the facts that you need to know about special education law.

STEP FOUR

Know Your
Legal Rights

CHAPTER SEVEN
UNDERSTAND THE LAW

I will never forget the first time I participated in a special education hearing, file folder in hand, anxious to testify for a bright 12-year-old young man whose teachers had simply stopped believing he would ever read at grade level. When it was over, the look of elation on the faces of his parents told the whole story. Properly understood and applied, the law works.

Most students who receive help in school from a reading specialist get that help through special education. The special education law was originally passed in 1975 for the purpose of providing a public education for all children with disabilities from the ages of 3 through 21. The law has been revised several times over the years. While I am not claiming to be an expert on the special education law, and its still undetermined changes, I offer the following information to parents.

INDIVIDUALS WITH DISABILITIES EDUCATION IMPROVEMENT ACT 2004 (IDEA 2004)

The most current version of the law, known as Individuals with Disabilities Education Improvement Act 2004 (IDEA 2004), is a federal law that applies to *all states and to all public schools*. The federal regulations that accompany the law add to and explain the law. Individual states have also each enacted their own state laws and regulations. Although individual states may exceed the standards set forth in the federal law, all states must *at least* meet the requirements of IDEA 2004. It is important for you to have a basic understanding of your state's law and regulations as you interact with your school to make decisions about your child's education. While you do not need to become an expert in the law, you will find it helpful to understand your rights.

IDEA 2004 and its regulations establish rules for educating children with disabilities and set procedural safeguards for children and their parents that schools are required to follow. The purpose of the law is to provide children with disabilities a *"free, appropriate public education"* (FAPE) to meet their unique needs and prepare them

> **FACT: A free, appropriate public education (FAPE)** is guaranteed by federal law (IDEA 2004) to all children with disabilities between the ages of 3 and 21.

for further education, employment, and independent living. This means that children are entitled to a free public education and their education must be appropriate to their needs, so they are able to learn.

School districts are also required to educate children with disabilities in the *"least restrictive environment."* This means that children with disabilities must be educated to the maximum extent appropriate in mainstream education classrooms with nondisabled children *unless they require a different environment to meet their educational needs.* The intent is to integrate children with special needs so they can benefit from a mainstream education. If, however, your child is not learning to read in the mainstream classroom and requires individual or small-group specialized reading instruction outside the classroom to be able to learn, he has the right to that instruction.

Children with reading problems have *several placement options, depending on how far behind grade-level their reading skills are, the severity of their problem, and whether they have any other disabilities that interfere with their learning.* Some children receive instruction in the mainstream classroom, while others may leave the mainstream classroom for small group or 1:1 tutoring if needed in order to learn. Students with more severe reading problems or those significantly behind their classmates may be placed in a self-contained language-based classroom in their school district, or they may attend a special school where they receive specialized instruction.

> **TIP:** If your child is not learning to read with the curriculum in the classroom, he has the right to instruction appropriate to his needs and in a location where he can learn.

READING HELP

IDEA 2004, together with another federal law also enacted in 2004, the *Elementary and Secondary Education Act*, a bill more commonly known as *No Child Left Behind (NCLB)*, sets clear regulations for students who receive reading help under special education. Schools are required to provide instruction using evidence-based methods of reading. Reading teachers are required to have expertise in reading. As you recall, evidence-based reading instruction is a method proven to be effective for teaching children who struggle to read. A more complete discussion of evidence-based reading instruction appears in Chapter 6.

REFERRALS FOR SPECIAL EDUCATION

According to IDEA 2004, the first step in getting special education help for a child is to initiate the referral process. Any adult who is involved in the life of a child may refer him for help. Most referrals come from teachers or parents.

If you believe your child needs help with reading, I recommend that you first speak with his teacher to find out how he is doing in class.

Is the teacher seeing what you are seeing? Has the teacher tried any special reading programs with your child? If so, is your child making progress? If not, has the teacher taken steps to begin a referral for an evaluation? Find out if his teacher has initiated the *response to intervention (RTI)* process.

You can refer your child for help by writing a letter addressed to the principal of your child's school and copying the director of special education on the letter. State the reasons for your request. Make sure you put this request *in writing* and date your letter. Keep a copy for your files. Your written request will trigger the special education process. The school is required to respond to your request within a set time limit. The time period may vary by state. If your child attends a private, religious, or charter school, or if he is homeschooled, you are entitled to the same rights and should follow the same process.

> **ACT:** To refer your child for reading help, write a letter to the principal of your child's school and copy the director of special education. State the reasons for your request. See www.SmartKidCantRead.com for sample letters.

If you are not sure if your child is at grade level, you can administer the informal tests found in the appendices of this book and at www.SmartKidCantRead.com. This may be a helpful tool if you are concerned that you are second-guessing yourself. Often parents are made to feel they are being overprotective or are "helicopter parents." These tools will give you a general indication of whether you are on the right track in voicing your concerns.

EVALUATIONS

Under IDEA 2004, schools are required to evaluate children to determine their eligibility for special education services. The law requires that they test in all areas of suspected disability and do not rely on just one test. Before the district can test your child, the school must obtain written consent from you. Once you have signed this consent, the school is required to complete the evaluation

> **FACT:** Students with reading difficulty are usually identified as having a "specific learning disability" for purposes of special education classification.

within a specified period of time. The time varies with different states, so check out the law in your state. The school is required to write a report explaining the test results.

For purposes of special education classification, students with reading disabilities are usually identified as having a "specific learning disability" unless the student has other disabilities that interfere with learning. This classification entitles your child to special education reading services and provides you and your child with rights under IDEA 2004. Two thirds (2/3) of all children who receive special education services in the country are classified as having "specific learning disabilities." The vast majority of those with this classification have reading problems.

Remember, *schools are not diagnostic facilities.* Schools test *to determine a child's eligibility for special education services;* they do not diagnose your child's strengths and weaknesses. School personnel generally lack diagnostic expertise, and some schools may have an inherent conflict of interest for making appropriate recommendations. For example, a school will not recommend a specialized reading program designed for dyslexic students if they do not have a teacher trained in the program. They are not likely to recommend one-on-one instruction or instruction of appropriate length if they have a shortage of trained reading teachers. Be aware that the school's recommendations must be based on your child's needs to make progress, not on what the school district has available.

Go outside your school system for your own diagnostic evaluation (see Chapter 3 for this discussion). The timing of your private evaluation depends on whether you plan to

ACT: Check with your school district to learn the procedure for public funding of an outside evaluation.

request public funding for the evaluation. School districts will pay for outside evaluations in certain circumstances for families who disagree with the results of the district's evaluation.

If you plan to request that the school fund your outside evaluation, check with your school district first to learn their procedure. You generally need to *let them test first.* If you disagree with their test results, you may then request an outside evaluation at public expense. However, if you plan to pay for your own evaluation, it is often better that you do that *before* the school does their testing. Many tests that the psy-

TIP: When your *state* law provides more benefits to your child than the *federal* law, you are guaranteed the better deal.

chologist will want to administer can be administered only once every 12 months. If the school has administered that particular test, then your psychologist cannot do so for another year.

For more information about the special education regulations in your particular state, please visit the website for your state's Department of Special Education. Remember that in cases where the state law provides more benefits to your child than the federal law, you are guaranteed the better deal.

INDIVIDUALIZED EDUCATION PROGRAM (IEP)

Under IDEA 2004, each child who receives special education help is required to have an *individualized education program (IEP)*. The IEP is a document that outlines the amount of help and the types of services your child will receive. You will meet with his teachers and other staff members to agree on—and write—the IEP for your child. Your input is essential when writing this document. An IEP is usually written for 1 year. However, you can request that it be revised or revoked at any time. This is important if you feel that your child is not progressing as expected. *You can withdraw your consent to all or parts of the IEP at any time.*

The IEP will have a statement about your child's *current level of functioning in reading*. This section should provide a clear statement of your child's current reading ability in all six areas of a reading evaluation. Make certain that standardized tests are used so you can measure progress at the end of the year. Make sure this statement includes test scores in the following areas:

1. Phonological processing

2. Decoding

3. Reading comprehension

4. Written language

5. Reading fluency

6. Spelling

The test scores from these six areas will serve as a baseline to measure your child's reading progress over the year.

The IEP will also include a statement of *measurable annual goals.* These should be the goals that you and the rest of the team realistically expect your child to achieve over the year. Use the scores from the current level of performance to set the standards for measurable annual goals. Request that the school utilize the same tests used for *current level of performance* and insist on appropriate growth with an effective reading program. If your child is of average intelligence with no other disabilities, it is reasonable to expect 1–2 years of growth. Recall that if your child is below grade level, he will need to make more than 1 year's progress in a school year if he is to close the reading gap and attain grade-level skills in reading. Comparing standard scores and percentile ranks is the best method for measuring performance over the year. That will show you whether your child is closing the gap between his performance and that of his peers. Review Chapter 4 for a more comprehensive discussion of how to monitor progress.

> **TIP:** If your child is of average intelligence and has no other disabilities, he should make at least 1 year's progress in a year. If your child is below grade level, he will need to make more than 1 year's progress in a year to close the gap between his performance and that of his peers.

The IEP may also include a statement regarding your child's *participation in state- or district-wide testing.* Your school may suggest that your child receive accommodations or alternative testing to pass these tests. These "high-stakes" tests are required in most states and are administered each year. Accommodations often include having the test read to your child and having a "scribe" write the answers for your child.

The results of your child's performance on these high-stakes tests are an opportunity for you to see how he performs relative to his peers in his classroom, his school, his school district, and his state. This is particularly important information if you are concerned that your child is not doing as well as his teachers suggest. For elementary school children I do not recommend that you permit the school to read test questions or scribe answers for your child.

You want to stay focused on getting your child the reading help he needs while he is still in the lower grades. Allowing him to be helped on the test may inflate his score and give everyone the impression that he is doing better than is actually the case. Aren't you already having enough trouble convincing people of his need for help? Warning! This advice is controversial, and you must make the best decision for your own child. Your school district may disagree with you and accuse you of putting pressure on your child.

Matt was an 11-year-old fifth grader approximately 2 years below grade-level in his reading skills. The school was unwilling to provide him with 1:1 reading help and, instead, gave him help twice per week in a group of six students. They stated that he did not need 1:1 help because there were other children in his class with similar delays and his delays were not severe enough. However, his IEP team recommended that he receive accommodations on the state-mandated testing at the end of the year. They wanted to provide him with someone who would sit with him individually and who would read test passages and questions to him and write his answers for him. His parents objected, stating that if he was not severe enough to receive individual help then he should not need individual assistance to take the test. Since the school did not provide him with a reader and a scribe in the classroom, his parents saw *no reason to provide him with that support for the test. They also reasoned that if someone read him the test, it would no longer be a test of **reading** comprehension, but a test of **listening** comprehension. The team chairperson told them that this would cause Matt too much stress. Later that evening, the principal called them at home to state that this was a terrible decision and they were harming their son. Matt's parents decided the real harm was being done by not providing him with the help he needed to learn to read. They remained firm in their decision to not "take the school off the hook."*

Test accommodations become a different issue for children in *middle school and high school*. Your child will likely be required to pass the test to graduate. There are other issues to consider as children get older, and test accommodations are usually beneficial for your child at this stage.

> **WARNING:** Granting permission for your school to administer alternative tests or to provide accommodations on high-stakes tests when your child is in elementary school may result in inflated scores.

TEAM MEETINGS

Under IDEA 2004, your child's special education team includes you as a participating and contributing member. As parents, you are automatically members of this team, along with the team chairperson, and your child's teachers who are relevant to his reading problem. Your principal, the school psychologist, and director of special education may or may not be there. Together, the team will consider the results of the battery of tests administered and determine your child's eligibility for services, including:

- How often your child will receive help

- How long each session should last

- Where your child will receive this help (in the classroom or perhaps in the learning center)

- Whether your child's reading sessions will be 1:1 or in a small group

- The type of reading help your child will receive

Remember, *you are an important part of the team!* The school district is required to make every reasonable attempt to include

> **TIP:** Sign only those parts of your child's IEP that you agree with.

you in the meetings. They may not make any decisions about your child without your consent. All decisions made about your child must include you as part of the process. If you show up at a meeting only to discover that all of the decisions have already been made, do not sign anything unless you agree. You deserve the right to provide input. You can agree to all of the IEP or parts of the IEP. If you believe there are portions of the IEP that do not meet the needs of your child, you can reject those portions.

PREPARATION FOR TEAM MEETINGS

Once the school has completed their evaluation of your child, they will convene a team meeting to discuss the results of their testing. Your child's test results will be reviewed, and decisions will be made regarding the type of help he will receive. You need to be prepared to discuss those results at the meeting because they will determine whether your child is eligible for special education reading help, what kind of help he receives, and how often he receives it. You need to request copies of the school's evaluation *in writing prior to the meeting*. Many schools will not give you the test results prior to the meeting *unless you request them*. Study these reports and come prepared with questions and comments. You do not want to be in the position of trying to read reports at the last minute in

> **TIP:** Request copies of the school's evaluation in writing prior to the team meeting.

the middle of the meeting. The school will be using the results of those evaluations to make recommendations about your child. You need to have an equal advantage in advocating your points.

It is particularly useful to bring your independent evaluator to a team meeting once her report is completed. You need your evaluator to explain her test results and her recommendations. The school is required to convene a meeting to discuss and consider that independent report. Depending upon when you have the independent evaluation done, this may or may not happen at the first meeting.

Many parents find it helpful to bring an advocate to a meeting, particularly if they anticipate any disagreement over the amount and type of reading help their child should receive. Special education advocates are trained in IDEA 2004 and in your state's special education law. They can help to make certain your child receives the help to which he is legally entitled. They also know how to work with school systems to help you get the help that your child needs. A good advocate can make a difference in the services your child receives because she understands the politics of your school system. Select an advocate who has experience with your particular school district.

TIPS FOR PREPARING FOR TEAM MEETINGS

Never go alone. If you do not have a spouse who can accompany you, bring a knowledgeable friend.

Bring your own evaluator to explain her findings and recommendations once her evaluation is completed.

Request copies of the school's evaluation reports before the meeting if the school has tested your child.

Study all reports before the meeting and write down your questions, comments, and requests for services.

Bring an advocate to the meeting if you anticipate any disagreement over your child's need for reading help.

Prepare a written statement of concerns and an action plan.

RESPONSE TO INTERVENTION (RTI)

RTI is a tiered educational program designed to identify struggling students early to provide appropriate instruction, and prevent the need to refer children for special education. Over the years it has become clear that many students who receive reading help in special education are not in fact learning disabled. Rather, they never received appropriate reading instruction in the beginning stages of learning to read. RTI is an attempt to provide these struggling readers with appropriate instruction without referring them to special education. The hope is that it will provide the needed help in a more timely way, without waiting for the long process required for special education services or waiting for a student to fall far enough behind to merit special services. In theory, this is a great idea.

There is wide variability in how RTI is implemented. In fact, I have never seen two programs that look alike. In general, RTI is a tiered program, in which Tier 1 is the general educational curriculum in the classroom. As a result of an initial screening, "at-risk" students may then be placed in Tier 2, where they receive more intensive and specialized reading instruction. Reading instruction must be "evidence-based" instruction taught by appropriately trained teachers. Students in the second tier are carefully monitored, and their progress is charted. If they do not respond to this instruction, they move on to Tier 3, with more intensive and a different type of instruction. This continues until

> **TIP:** RTI may not be used to deny or delay referral for special education. Parents may still request an evaluation for special education.

ultimately students are either successful and returned to the general curriculum or referred to special education. A student's response to the instruction or intervention is used to make decisions such as eligibility for special education and type of instruction.

When used correctly, RTI has the potential for helping children who struggle with reading but who do not have specific learning disabilities. When used incorrectly, RTI can delay or deny help to students who need it. Unfortunately, many independent evaluators report that progress monitoring reported by some schools in these programs can be misleading and inflate the child's reading ability. RTI may not be used to deny or delay referral for special education. You may still request an evaluation for special education.

> **WARNING:** Monitor your child's education under RTI.

It is important that you monitor your child's education under RTI. Ask questions about the reading curriculum and the training of the teacher in the use of that curriculum. Find out how progress is monitored and what the goals are for your child.

PRIVATE, RELIGIOUS, CHARTER SCHOOLS AND HOMESCHOOLING

Students who are homeschooled or who attend private or religious schools present different issues from students in public schools. The regulations for these students vary according to the state law. IDEA 2004 provides that children who are homeschooled or who attend private or religious schools are entitled to receive the same services they would receive if they attended the public school. Children who attend charter schools are also entitled to the same services given to students in the rest of the school district. (Remember that charter schools are public schools.) If you are the parent of a child who is homeschooled or enrolled in a private or religious school, you are legally entitled to and can initiate the special education process through the public school system by requesting an evaluation *at the school your child would have attended in the public school system.*

Once your child has been identified by your public school system, he is eligible to receive services. The location and extent of those services vary from state to state and community to community.

> **FACT:** Children in private, religious, or home schools can receive special education services under federal law.

In some areas, the public school may provide an in-school tutor for your child in the private setting. In other areas, your child will receive help at the public school for a portion of the school day.

Parents of children in private, religious, or home schools should follow the same procedure outlined for students in public schools. Begin by meeting with the building principal of the school your child would have been assigned to if he attended your local public school. Submit a written request for a special education evaluation. As with children who attend the public school system, the law mandates that once you have made the request, the school must respond to your request. The school will likely evaluate your child. If you disagree with the school district's evaluation results, you may request an independent evaluation at public expense. Once again, I recommend that you obtain your own private, diagnostic evaluation.

PROCEDURAL SAFEGUARDS AND AREAS OF DISAGREEMENT

The special education law provides a series of procedural safeguards the school district and parents must follow to ensure that the child receives a "free, appropriate public education." There are also provisions in the law for instances when the parents and school district disagree about the help the child should receive. While a discussion of these safeguards is beyond the scope of this overview, it is important that you understand them if you find yourself in a disagreement with your school system. The school administrators will know the law, and you should be familiar with it.

If you find yourself in a stalemate with your school, I recommend that you engage a special education advocate. While advocates usually are not lawyers, they are trained in the law and have considerable experience working with school systems. If you have to go to a special education hearing, I recommend that you hire a special education attorney with expertise in this area.

Knowing the law does not require an in-depth knowledge of complicated processes. Be aware of the terms in this chapter. Know that you and your child have rights as citizens. Resolve to advocate for your child so he will have the education guaranteed by law.

STEP FIVE

Advocate for Your Child

CHAPTER EIGHT

BECOME A MOTHER BEAR

"When you negotiate with the school on your child's behalf, you increase the odds that your child will get an appropriate education. You cannot leave this job to others!"[31]

—Pam Wright and Pete Wright
Authors of *Emotions to Advocacy:
The Special Education Survival Guide*

Gayle Walker became one of the most effective parent advocates I have known. The Walkers contacted me at the beginning of the school year, anxious to find a way to help their 10-year-old son. The family adopted Timothy when he was less than a week old. Having grown up in a calm environment, the couple was unprepared for the unbridled energy and rule testing that Timothy displayed as he entered the preschool years. Obtaining a diagnosis of attention-deficit/ hyperactivity disorder (ADHD) long before it was a household word, the Walkers thought they had gotten to the root of their son's issues. As one school year melded into the next, however, Gayle's concerns increased. Although Timothy's teachers

---

31   *From Emotions to Advocacy: The Special Education Survival Guide* (p. xiv), by P. Wright and P. Wright, 1992, Hartfield, VA: Harbor House Law Press.

never indicated there was a problem, Gayle began to notice patterns she found troubling. Timothy loved building complex vehicles with Legos, and he was good at anything mechanical. However, he had to work overtime on his schoolwork, a source of much household stress. The Walkers sat with their son at the table for hours doing homework, with Timothy exclaiming, "I'm FLUSTATED!" Spelling papers came back with rows of red "x's" and teacher admonitions about the importance of studying.

"It's not just that he's making spelling errors," Gayle told me, pushing his worksheets and papers across the desk. "Look at them. The errors don't make any sense. It's like he's not hearing all the sounds or something."

Indeed. As I scanned through one of Timothy's social studies papers, I noticed that he dropped off blends, writing "sedy beet" for "steady beat" and "latin" for "lantern." "His reading is problematic as well," Gayle continued. "He has trouble when there are a lot of sounds in a word and sometimes drops off whole parts of longer words."

Thumbing through the worksheets, it became clear to me why the family had been experiencing so much stress. "Has the school evaluated him for a learning disability?" I asked Gayle.

It was then that I discovered that Gayle had no idea of her rights under the law. I provided her with several booklets explaining the services guaranteed to all children in the United States under the federal law, Individuals with Disabilities Education Improvement Act 2004 (IDEA 2004), and advised Gayle to contact her building principal to request an initial evaluation through the school system to determine Timmy's *eligibility for special education services. I explained that, if she ultimately disagreed with the school's evaluation results, she was eligible for the school district to pay for an independent evaluation—but she must first allow them to test her son. I did not hear from the family for 4 months.*

When Gayle next entered my office she was clearly rattled. Following through on my advice, she had typed a letter and mailed it to the principal. After more than a month of waiting for a response, Gayle eventually received a letter informing her that the school would test Timmy. Two months later, they scheduled a meeting to discuss the test results—on a date that Gayle was scheduled to work. Things went from bad to worse as she tried to explain to the secretary at the school that she desperately needed an alternate date. Feeling as if she had started off on the wrong foot, Gayle arrived at the rescheduled meeting alone and totally unfamiliar with school policies. She walked into the room and did not recognize anyone at the table except for her child's fourth grade teacher and the principal.

FACT: Schools must make every effort to accommodate parents' schedules in planning a meeting and provide a formal meeting notice, listing the date, time, location, and the names and roles of all participants.

"I felt like an outsider," she told me. "The principal sat on one side of me. The special education teacher sat on the other side. There was a school psychologist and a speech and language specialist across from me. I don't know . . . I just felt overwhelmed. Kind of like they thought I was overreacting to my son's problems or something." Then came the ultimate blow.

"It was an open-and-shut case," she said. "They told me Timmy was fine. They spread some tests on the table and quickly reviewed the case. Timothy is a low-average student. He is doing what can be expected. His report cards show that he is making progress." Gayle shifted in her chair and then faced me with a look of despair. "I know there's more to the story than that. I just felt so confused that I didn't know what to say. I don't even know where to go from here."

I advised Gayle to notify the school in writing that she disagreed with their findings and was requesting public funding for an independent evaluation.

It is easy to be intimidated by the school system, especially when you are unclear about the rules and the players. If you are to interact effectively, it is important to understand the structure of your system before entering the playing field. Take some time to investigate the organizational structure that forms the basis for decision making in your system. Who are the gatekeepers? How are financial decisions made? Who determines the type of reading instruction students receive? Entering a room with a clear understanding of each person's role is the first step to appearing confident and relaxed. Here are some other basic rules of the road:

MANAGING TEAM MEETINGS

1. **Never go to a team meeting alone.** *Gayle was surprised to discover a new feeling in the room when she returned to a follow-up meeting with her husband and an advocate. "Suddenly, it was no longer me against the world," she said. "I felt supported. I began to speak up and they started taking me seriously."*

I always advise both parents to attend meetings. This is true regardless of whether you are currently married. If your child's other parent is unable to accompany you to the meeting, find someone to go with you, preferably someone who is a good note-taker. If possible, select someone who knows the field of education. At the very least, bring someone who exudes confidence. As a courtesy, you should notify the team chairperson that you are bringing a guest or guests, but you are not required to identify the role of anyone who will be attending the meeting with you. If you are bringing a lawyer, the district must be notified and is permitted to reschedule so that their attorney can attend. Remember, you are totally within your rights to show up at a meeting with anyone you would like to have with you.

Initially, Gayle's husband did not want to go with her. He did not like taking time off from work and felt he had nothing to offer. After all, Gayle was in charge of the children, and what happened at school was Gayle's responsibility. But once Gayle convinced him to attend, things changed.

"He didn't say a lot at the meeting," Gayle told me. "But when he spoke, everyone listened. They treated us with a lot more respect because he was there."

Recall that you want to bring an advocate to the meeting if you anticipate a disagreement over the help your child needs. Bring your independent evaluator to the meeting to explain your child's evaluation results when that evaluation is completed or convene another meeting.

2. **Be prepared for the meeting.** Most team chairpersons work from an agenda. Ask for a copy of the agenda in advance of the

meeting. Make sure the items you want to discuss are included. You want to know who will be in attendance and what part each person will play in the meeting. Remember, you are an equal participant in your child's team meetings.

Make certain you have all the documents you will need. It is important that you have written copies of the school's evaluation reports ahead of time if they have completed an evaluation of your child. Study those reports and come prepared with a written list of questions.

3. **Know what you want.** Before entering the meeting, decide what actions you want team members to take. If your evaluator or advocate will be attending with you, confer with him or her prior to the scheduled date. Be clear on your goals. What is your bottom line? What is negotiable? What are you unwilling to relinquish? Does your child need daily instruction in a pull-out setting with 1:1 help in reading? Is there a particular type of instruction that will benefit him? To make these decisions, you must be informed about what your child needs. That information will come from your independent evaluation.

    Study the chapters in this book that will make you a strong advocate for your child. Know the law (Chapter 7). Understand the basics of sound reading instruction (Chapters 5 and 6). Get an independent evaluation that informs you about the needs of your child (Chapters 3 and 4).

    Some advocates recommend that parents prepare a written

    > **TIP:** As a well-informed parent, you will accomplish more than the parent who is dependent on school staff to reveal and interpret what is most important.

Statement of Concerns and a Request for Services that list each area of difficulty along with the services their child needs. Bring copies for each team member, and make sure that your requests for services receive a formal response.

4. **Take the time you need to make an informed decision.** Make certain you have the information you need in order to make the best, most informed decision for your child. *Gayle's team eventually recommended that Timmy receive reading instruction three times per week in a reading group with two other students. Gayle requested that I observe the group before agreeing to the placement. In fact, we discovered the other boys had behavioral issues and their reading skills were much higher than Timmy's. Gayle and I went through the process of evaluating several other options before deciding on the right placement for Timmy.*

When assessing programs, the goal is to determine if the reading services being recommended meet your child's needs. Even the best program in the world is not effective if it does not happen to be the particular program *your* child needs. As you investigate class-rooms, look around at the students. Do they show a similar profile

> **WARNING:** Even the best program in the world is not effective if it is not the particular program *your* child needs.

to your child? If the program is a good match, you will find that the other students in the reading and language arts groups are at, or close to, your child's instructional level.

Remember that you can accept all or parts of the IEP. If there are particular areas that you believe do not meet the needs of your child, you can reject those portions of the IEP.

5. **Be respectful.** While the language of this book is that of advocacy, be careful not to come across as militant. Your first job is to prepare for a team meeting as if you are doing homework for an actual class. Your second job is to present yourself as composed, confident, and friendly. Be willing to listen as well as to advocate your points. Research has found that effective communicators know when to entertain another's point of view and when to advance their own. Be open to the ideas being shared around the table. Remember that each person has a unique perspective to offer. As the parent, you have known your child from the day he was born. You have the perspective of history. Your child's teacher has the perspective of age-appropriate expectations. Teachers also see your child in the context of his peers. Special educators come to the table with information on your child's performance on specific tests. They have the perspective of your child's ability relative to his peers. Working as a team, your job is to piece together the complex picture of your child and what will best help him learn to read.

Gayle did not agree with the school's initial finding that Timmy did not have a learning disability, but she remained respectful. When you disagree, you must be prepared to explain the reasons for your disagreement and have test results and research data to back up your position. Gayle got an independent evaluation that confirmed Timmy's reading disability. That evaluation gave her the information she needed to get services for Timmy.

6. **Actively look for ways to validate the positive things happening in your child's classroom.** In general, teachers work very

hard to meet the varied demands of the job. Though you must enter a team meeting with the energy it takes to fully advocate for your child, be sensitive to the honest efforts on the part of team members. Don't engage in blaming. In nearly all cases, teachers are doing the best they can. Take the time to articulate what you appreciate about the school's efforts. Philosophical differences about reading instruction as well as financial issues often dictate the type of reading curriculum in your local school district and the type of training your child's teacher has received. People hold strong beliefs about how best to teach reading. You may be challenging deeply held convictions.

As you speak up for your child, be aware that some teachers may interpret your questions as an encroachment on their territory. Reassure the team that you are not questioning their professionalism. You simply want to work together with all parties in order to come to the best solution for the very unique needs of *your* child.

7. **Become an informed parent.** Recognize that while administrators do not like parents to question their decisions about curriculum and instruction, they do come to respect parents who speak from a backdrop of understanding. Once again, you have a very fine line to walk. Learn the federal law and your state's special education regulations. Some states have higher standards than IDEA 2004, so educating yourself levels the playing field between you and other members of the team discussing your child.

With a clear understanding of your child and his educational needs, you will have the knowledge base needed to leverage your position. You do not have to be unpleasant. You do not have to be insulting. *You do have to be taken seriously.* The goal is to establish an atmosphere of mutual respect. As you reveal your depth of *understanding of the law, the reading process, and your own child,* you will position yourself as a valuable member of the team. Stay clear on the purpose of the meeting. You are there to find solutions for your child. Armed with an arsenal of accurate information, expect to be treated as a worthwhile contributor at the table.

Initially Gayle lacked the confidence to put forward Timmy's case and relied on her advocate and evaluator to do this. As the team gained respect for one another and developed a working relationship, she became increasingly able to speak up and make her case on her own.

> **TIP:** With a clear understanding of your child and his needs, you will have the knowledge needed to leverage your position.

8. **Leave your strong emotions at home.** A team meeting is not the place to break down in tears or engage in a yelling match. Preparing for the meeting not only involves doing your homework on the language of the law, the roles of the players, and understanding your child's needs, but also means acknowledging and processing your own emotions in advance. Know your own style under stress. Do you tend to clam up when the pressure mounts, fearful of saying something you will regret? On the other hand, do you find yourself speaking in angry tones, raising your voice when the stakes get high?

Take time to talk things through with a trusted friend or family member in advance. Work through any anger or disappointment you may be experiencing. Know your own "hot spots."

Practice staying focused on your "talking points" without suc-
cumbing to emotional tides. Be clear on the reason for your high
level of involvement. You are about to
enter a meeting to advocate for your
child. Stay focused on the present and
the decisions that need to be made now.
Don't indulge in historical recrimina-

> **TIP:** Work through your emotions at home before entering a team meeting.

tions. What is past may well have contributed to your current
dilemma, but it does no good to indulge in anger over it. Move
forward.

*Mike's parents could not let their anger go. They were
furious about the school's refusal to give Mike appropriate
reading instruction in the early grades, the inadequate Band-
Aid treatments they provided in third and fourth grades, and
their son's continued inability to read in fifth grade. This had
led to some serious emotional issues for Mike. Their team
meetings were a series of angry exchanges between parents
and school personnel. Everyone seemed to be stuck in the past.
In part Mike's parents were angry with themselves. As they
became more informed, they realized what they should have
done earlier. Because they had trouble moving forward, they
were less effective.*

You will know you are emotionally ready for the meeting when
you are able to view yourself, the teachers, and school officials as
members of the same team. Preparing your itemized Statement
of Concerns and Request for Services will help you stay focused
and remind you what needs to be accomplished.

Standing up for your child is not an easy task. It means rolling up your sleeves and doing the hard work. It means being the parent who will not go away. It means late nights studying the law. Preparation. Persistence. Perseverance. Like the Walkers, you can interact with your child's school system in the educated, tireless manner that will get results.

GET ORGANIZED

You will soon realize that you are drowning in paperwork. It is important to develop an organizational system if you want to stay on top of all the paperwork and meetings. You must keep records of all interactions, both written and oral, between you and the school. This includes all evaluation reports and individualized education programs (IEPs). Reports, evaluations, letters from schools, emails, schedules, and more . . . The list of documents will grow. If your situation becomes adversarial, these records will be essential because you will need documentation of all interactions. This is where the historical accuracy of your case becomes important.

Create a notebook dedicated to your child for each academic year. Maintain a record of everything that happens concerning your child's learning process. Develop a section of your notebook or a file folder that is devoted to each of the following areas:

1. Correspondence

  ▸ Document all conversations with your child's teachers, principal, team chairperson, or special education director. Make notes of the important interactions. Date all conversations.

  ▸ Print out and save all emails between you and the teachers, principal, or director of special education.

▸ Make copies of all signed letters regarding your child's education, and be sure that you have proof of delivery.

2. Report cards for the current year

3. The current IEP

4. All school testing

5. Private evaluations

6. A summary of all decisions made at team meetings, along with a summary of the interactions in the meeting

7. A sampling of your child's *unedited* work

8. A list of questions to ask the teacher, evaluator, and principal

Treat the process of getting your child services as if it were a job. At work you would be expected to keep papers filed and organized in order to locate items quickly. Make sure to send copies of written correspondence

> **ACT:** Create a notebook and a set of file folders for each academic year with sections for all documents, services, and interactions.

to people at different levels in your school system, such as the teacher, principal, director of special education, and superintendent.

Being organized takes time, but it is important in giving you a sense of control. Over and over again, I have seen overwhelmed parents come into my office, scrambling for the paperwork they received from the school, or shuffling through one big folder where everything has been dumped. When you are feeling distraught about a teacher's words or powerless against the system, being able to quickly find a piece of correspondence or your child's evaluation can help you regain control.

BUILD YOUR TEAM

Team building is a theme repeated throughout this book. While the school is one of your resources, you now realize that if your child is not making progress the school should not be your only resource. If you find yourself in disagreement with your school system, you cannot go it alone. As you have already learned, your school will not grant specialized reading services of the type your child needs and the amount of help he requires just because you ask for it. You need to build your case by providing convincing data to support your request for reading help.

The most effective parent advocate teams usually include:

▶ Both parents

▶ A special education advocate

▶ The professionals who completed your independent evaluations

Let's consider the role that each of these individuals will play. First, the presence of both parents is important for your success with the team. If you are unable to bring your child's other parent, bring a trusted friend. You need support and a second set of eyes and ears to take detailed notes and to help you process what is happening.

Second, an advocate can be extremely helpful if you are having difficulty convincing the school of your child's needs. Advocates know special education law and make certain that your rights and the rights of your child are not violated. They frequently are familiar with many of the educational issues in your school system and understand why your child is having difficulty. I frequently refer parents to advocates. They can say what needs to be said when parents are reluctant to be direct. When deciding on an advocate, be sure to be clear on the rates that will be charged. Even if you hire someone, you must educate yourself and learn to advocate for your own child. The advocate cannot replace the role of the parent. All decision-making power ultimately rests with the parent.

Third, your team should include a professional with credentials respected by the school, one who has evaluated your child and documented his need for specialized reading help. This independent evaluator can make the case to the school regarding the type of help

> **FACT:** Decision-making power regarding your child's education ultimately rests with you.

your child needs, how often he needs help, and for what length of time. Consider hiring the independent evaluator to attend team meetings when decisions will be made based on test results and recommendations. Some evaluators include this in their fees for evaluation; clarify the terms of the arrangement at the first meeting. If the district has any questions about the independent evaluator's report or recommendations, these concerns should be addressed during the team meeting.

As you build your team, keep in mind that advocates and independent evaluators can be used in different ways. Often both the evaluator and advocate attend the initial meetings until the IEP has been written. Some parents ask either the advocate or evaluator to attend each meeting with them even after decisions have been made. Others ask the evaluator or advocate to attend meetings whenever services are being changed on the individualized education program. Remember, most IEPs are rewritten every year. The way in which you utilize your team really depends on your need for support. Some school systems are easier to work with than others. If you are attempting to work with a school system that is resistant to your input, you will need a considerable amount of support.

NETWORK WITH OTHER PARENTS

By now you realize that you are not alone. There are dozens of other families in your community who are going through the same thing. Find them. Some of these families do not yet realize they need to advocate for their children. Others are ahead of you in their journey and are experienced in the process.

These families can provide you with resources, advice, and support. Many of them will know the ropes and can give you good advice about the people in your school system. It is from these parents that you will learn who the best tutors are and which evaluators will do classroom observations or attend team meetings. You will learn which advocates have working relationships with your school system and which ones know how to help you get what your child needs.

> **TIP:** You are not alone. Find the other families in your community who are going through the same thing.

FIND YOUR VOICE

Never assume the educational leaders in your school system know about the reading research that validates the use of evidence-based reading programs. You will soon learn that many do not understand the consequences of inadequate reading instruction. Others may be unfamiliar with the federal special education law (IDEA 2004). Many teachers and school administrators went to school when colleges were teaching the whole language philosophy. Often, colleges and universities continue to teach this philosophy, keeping young teachers unaware of evidence-based reading instruction. We are asking these teachers to adopt new teaching strategies that run counter to their deeply held beliefs that children should be able to learn to read by mere exposure to the written word.

Become an agent of change by helping educators in your school system learn about research-based reading instruction. Provide members of your school committee, administrators, and teachers with articles and books that will educate them. Bring in speakers to talk about this issue with your parent-teacher association. Use your parent-teacher association to raise money to train teachers in evidence-based reading programs.

Write to your school committee and principal to ask what reading curriculum is being used in your school. How was the decision made to select this curriculum? Do the selected programs include the evidence-based characteristics discussed in Chapter 6? How have teachers been trained in the use of this specialized instruction?

Continue to educate yourself. This book is your start—but keep going. Use your information and the law to bring about change in your system. Organize with other parents to demand an evidence-based reading curriculum and teacher training.

> **ACT:** Become an agent of change in your community. When you organize with other parents you can have a profound impact on your school system.

PARENT POWER

When parents organize, they can have a profound impact on their school system. If you believe your school system needs systemic change in teaching reading, then you need to collaborate with other parents. Over and over again, I have seen firsthand the power of parents. You are ultimately in control of your local school system, and you cannot be ignored. Parent power is particularly effective when it is organized.

I have seen groups of parents in several communities come together to change their special education departments. They lobbied and educated individual school committee members and testified at meetings about their concerns with the reading programs being used to help struggling readers. They insisted on programs that were effective and research-based.

I have seen groups of parents work through their parent advisory committees to raise money for teacher training in specialized reading programs. In one instance, when the director of special education refused to accept the money because she did not want parents interfering, they lobbied for her replacement.

I have worked with numerous parents who later became school board members. Being intimately involved in the workings of their school system, they were in a strong position to work for improved reading programs.

An even larger number of parents I have counseled have gone on to become special education advocates. They have made it their mission to help other parents.

As you think about the ways you can advocate for your own child, you will most likely find yourself helping others as well. Together, as parents, you can support and strengthen one another. You are in good company.

CHAPTER NINE

GET STARTED!

"Knowledge is power. I was able to help argue for the essential elements of reading instruction because I knew I had research and facts on my side. It is easy for educators or policy makers to discount your opinion if these don't agree with theirs. But it is far more difficult to ignore or reject reams of data and information that prove your opinions."[32]

Marion Joseph, grandmother and member
of California Department of Education
"When a Whole State Fails to Measure Up:
One Grandmother's Fight for Phonics"

Julie appeared in my office, speaking rapidly. "I don't think the school is telling me the truth." While her third-grade daughter, Savannah, struggled to read, every parent-teacher conference yielded the same message. Savannah was fine; she just needed a little time to catch up to her peers. Her teachers had been monitoring her reading progress monthly for the past year and a half and said that she was making significant progress. After 3 years of such messages, Julie was no longer buying it.

---

32 "When a Whole State Fails to Measure Up: One Grandmother's Fight for Phonics" by M. Joseph, in *Why Kids Can't Read: Challenging the Status Quo in Education* (p. 83), edited by P. Blaunstein & R. Lyon , Lanham, MD.: Rowman and Littlefield Education.

I listened closely to Julie's words while Savannah hung back, hiding behind her long, blond hair, eyes downcast. Julie's determined stance stood out in sharp contrast to her daughter's defeated posture. This mom was not going to stand idle anymore! Her intuition told her it was time to act. I would later discover that Savannah had a severe reading disability. Test results showed an early first grade reading level. Julie's maternal intuition had been right.

This was the beginning of my professional relationship with a family that would not give up. Over the ensuing weeks, Julie and Savannah drove more than 2 hours each way to meet me at my office. After I finished my evaluation, Julie and her husband, Tom, spent hours going over the report with me. We discussed each recommendation at length. The three of us entered the team meeting as a unified force. Savannah's parents understood what she needed and were willing to stay the course until they got it. Surrounded by a supportive extended family, buoyed up by an advocate, armed with information, the family ultimately persisted until Savannah became a successful reader. This took time and careful planning.

Initially, Savannah's school offered to place her in a self-contained language-based classroom for children with learning disabilities. When I visited the classroom, it became clear that the instruction was not language-based and there was no particular reading program. The children in the classroom had varied profiles, ranging from Down syndrome to autism to dyslexia. We rejected this placement and insisted that the school provide the kind of reading instruction Savannah needed in an appropriate learning environment. We advocated for more than

2 months until the school officials began to take us seriously. Under pressure, the school finally assented to our demands, placing Savannah in a classroom with a teacher trained in reading methods for children with learning disabilities. Her parents paid for private tutoring over the summer. After 2 years of hard work, Savannah was able to function successfully in a regular classroom.

Julie stayed on top of Savannah's academic program all the way through high school. She championed for extended time on tests, audio books, and class note-takers. While Savannah is still a slow reader and continues to struggle with spelling, she has graduated from high school, passed her SATs, and gone on to study nursing. More importantly, she is a poised and confident young woman who has come to believe that she can achieve her dreams.

Without reading help, Savannah would have continued to fall through the cracks, sliding further and further below her peers. Julie believes that her personal struggle to help her daughter is the single most important thing she could have ever done for her child.

BECOMING YOUR CHILD'S ADVOCATE

As you made your way through the pages of this book, you entered a journey that at times may have seemed daunting and perplexing. For the sake of your child, do not give up. While the school system must balance the needs of many children, you are the only one who can advocate for the unique needs of your own child. Let's review your five steps to success.

STEP ONE: ACT AS SOON AS YOU SUSPECT A PROBLEM

Chapters 1 and 2 are devoted to this essential concept. Chapter 1 provides insight into the reasons that schools tend to delay giving help to struggling readers and gives you ideas about how to manage this. Chapter 2 provides you with information to help you determine whether you child is reading at grade level.

You have read about the pervasiveness of reading problems and understand that your child can be helped. You have learned that the earlier a child receives intervention in reading, the better his chances of catching up. It's never too late and it's never too early.

> **TIP:** For the sake of your child, do not give up.

I am currently advising the mother of a kindergartener who is clearly struggling at the beginning stages of reading.

> **ACT:** Now is the time to act. It's never too late and it's never too early.

Kara's teachers have expressed their concerns to her parents. However, her school has nothing to offer her at such a young age. Her parents have wisely decided not to wait for the school. They will hire an Orton Gillingham tutor this summer to work with Kara. They have decided they will continue with this tutor for the first half of Kara's first grade year. If she is still behind her peers by midyear, they will initiate the process with the school for special education help.

Kara's parents recognized the signs indicating that their daughter was at risk for reading problems. They monitored the work papers she brought home from kindergarten and spoke with her teacher. They developed a plan for helping Kara and refused to wait for her to experience failure.

You have read a number of stories about children who were several years behind in reading. You have discovered that some parents get involved in seeking help in elementary school, some in middle school, and others in high school. While it's more difficult as children get older, remember that *it's never too late to get the help your child needs.*

If you are uncertain whether your child is reading at grade-level, you can administer the grade-level screening tests found in the appendices of this book and at www.SmartKidCantRead.com. These screening tests will give you a general idea of whether your concerns about your child's reading skills are justified.

STEP TWO: UNDERSTAND WHAT YOUR CHILD NEEDS

Chapters 3 and 4 explain how you can learn what your child needs. Your action plan is based on having *good information* regarding your child's needs—and *understanding* that information.

You have learned the importance of getting an evaluation outside the school system that provides information leading to an effective remediation plan. Remember, you need an evaluation that is not tied to a school budget or limited by the resources available in your community. You must understand what your child needs above and beyond what the school can provide, if you are to make progress in helping your child.

> **ACT:** Get a good **independent** evaluation to learn what your child needs.

You have also learned what should be included in a good evaluation and the importance of understanding test results. Again, you cannot continue to rely on others to interpret those results for you.

A professional, diagnostic evaluation from someone outside the school system, as discussed in depth in Chapter 3, is the backbone of your advocacy plan. This report will tell you and the school what your child's strengths and weaknesses are and will offer a specific course of action that will put your son or daughter on the path to becoming a good reader. The effectiveness and importance of this evaluation cannot be overstated.

Take your time in identifying the best professional in your area to conduct the evaluation. *Savannah's mom drove 2 hours, from Hartford, Connecticut, to Boston, Massachusetts, to avail herself of my services. In the end, her child's newly gained success in reading made it all worth it.*

Once you have identified the best private evaluator in your area and received his or her report, remember that it is necessary for you to understand exactly what the report says. Walk through each recommendation with your evaluator until you understand it. While you may already know many of your child's strengths and weaknesses, the best way to remediate or help your child academically may not be obvious. Meet with the evaluator before meeting with the school. Take notes and ask questions. Discover exactly what your child will need in order to be a successful reader. Learn to interpret test scores so that you know what those reports mean.

STEP THREE: LEARN ABOUT THE READING PROCESS

Chapters 5 and 6 are devoted to providing some basic background information about reading problems. You need to know what a good reading program looks like and why children struggle with reading.

Recall that while learning to speak is a natural process, reading is a very complex process that requires direct instruction for most of us. While there are some children who seem to learn to read "naturally," your child is not one of them. Like many others, she needs to be taught the "phonemes" or specific speech sounds of the English language and the letters that make these sounds. She then needs to go through an explicit, sequential program that will help her build on her knowledge of sounds, letters, and word parts.

Again, good readers *do not rely on guesswork.* Reading is a complicated process that involves several parts of the brain. Research shows that reading problems exist at all levels of intelligence; a reading problem does not mean that your child is not smart. There are many factors that lead to reading difficulty, but the failure of the school system to provide appropriate reading instruction in the early grades is the leading cause of reading problems.

> **FACT:** While learning to speak is a natural process, reading is a more complex process that requires explicit instruction for most students.

Know how your child is being taught, and then ask the question, "Is this the best method for my child to learn to read?" As outlined in Chapter 6, much research has been conducted on the most effective methods of teaching a child to read. It is important for you to know what is happening each day during the literacy block in your child's classroom. Begin by asking your child's teacher about the reading program. Read through your child's textbooks; look through her homework and workbooks.

How do you know whether the method used in your child's classroom is working for her? First, if your child isn't learning to read, then the program is not working for her. It is as simple as that! As a parent, your intuition has already alerted you to this.

Review Chapter 6 to get a clear picture of what effective reading instruction for struggling readers looks like. Then review your child's strengths and weaknesses as indicated by the professional evaluation.

Is there a match between the proposed reading program and your child's profile? The academic recommendations made in your child's evaluation should be used to select a structured reading program that meets the unique needs of your son or daughter.

Some of you may find yourselves in the middle of what appears to be a minefield. As you have read, many professionals are very passionate about the best way to teach reading. While some contend that a holistic sight-word approach leaves too many children behind, others believe phonics is a "drill and kill" routine. Despite legislation that mandates research-based reading programs, many school systems resist a structured phonics approach and believe in a more literature-based sight-word approach to reading. Unfortunately, you are caught in the middle of the "reading wars" when all you really care about is that they teach your child to read!

> As one father recently voiced at a team meeting, "I'm not asking for noneducational services here. I'm not asking for psychological help, free contraceptives, medical assistance... I'm asking you to teach Jim to read. Can you do that here?"

Ironically, while the budgets of school systems' special education departments are overwhelmed by having to provide special help to children who struggle with reading, they could easily avoid this problem by providing appropriate reading instruction in kindergarten through Grade 3. It is a problem of their own making, but, unfortunately, it is one with which you must contend.

Your child *can* learn to read with the right instruction; it is not too late. Your child may feel like there is no hope. This is your chance to help her experience academic success.

STEP FOUR: KNOW YOUR LEGAL RIGHTS

Most children who receive help in reading receive that help with a special education teacher. Chapter 7 provides an overview of the special education law, with an emphasis on the aspects of the law that are relevant to children who have difficulty reading.

Remember that being an informed parent advocate means knowing your child's educational rights. Individuals with Disabilities Education Improvement Act 2004 (IDEA 2004) outlines every student's

> **TIP:** Being an informed parent advocate means knowing your child's educational rights.

right to a free, and appropriate public education. Knowing what the law says will arm you with powerful information and help you when you are up against a difficult school system or feel overwhelmed by the whole process. Your child has the right to services.

In researching the law, it might be helpful to know that IDEA 2004 is available as a booklet. You can also print out the sections that are relevant to you. Savannah's mom began to carry a copy of IDEA 2004 into meetings, laying out her notes beside the booklet that explained her child's rights. The point was not lost on school officials! Julie was armed and informed. As you enter team meetings, consider carrying a folder of information, including IDEA 2004. This will alert those in decision-making roles that you are ready to take action on your child's behalf.

Often parents are afraid of mentioning their child's rights under the law for fear of upsetting the key figures who will ultimately decide on the services granted. Other parents assume that the principal and school system will automatically adhere to these laws simply because they exist. Remember that the school system is hamstrung with budgetary constraints and most will do everything they must do to stay within their budget—even if this means not providing your child with the help she needs. Know your rights, and let everyone in the system know you are aware of them.

STEP FIVE: ADVOCATE FOR YOUR CHILD

Chapters 8 and 9 provide tips to help you develop a successful plan for advocating for your child so that you can avoid some common pitfalls. These strategies are based on my experience of working with parents, advocates, and special education attorneys.

In more than 30 years of practice, having seen hundreds of students of all ages, I can tell you without hesitation that *children whose parents advocate on their behalf generally receive more help and better services than children whose parents do not advocate for them. Schools have limited resources, and you are competing for those resources.*

The process of getting your child the services she needs and deserves can take a long time; sometimes families wait an entire school

> **TIP:** Children whose parents advocate on their behalf generally receive more help and better services than children whose parents do not advocate for them.

year for an effective educational plan. Many parents express that advocating for their child is the hardest thing they have ever done. But without fail, these same parents quickly assert that it is all worth it in the end.

> *"It was an exhausting battle," one father told me. "At times, it seemed as if we were hitting one wall after another. But we couldn't just stand back and watch him fail. In the end, he marched down that graduation aisle with everyone else. We couldn't have been prouder."*

You know your child better than anyone. Your instincts have led you this far. Advocating for your child's needs can be emotional and stressful. At times you will feel isolated and begin to question your

> **ACT:** Surround yourself with people who believe in your child and have her best interests at heart.

own parental intuition. Surround yourself with people who also believe in your child and have her best interests at heart.

The power of networking cannot be overstated. Identify parents who have already started to walk the road; you will gain strength in knowing

---

FIVE STEPS TO BECOMING
AN EFFECTIVE ADVOCATE FOR YOUR CHILD

▶ **Don't Wait.** Trust your instincts and act as soon as you suspect a problem. Learn to recognize the signs indicating that your child may be struggling with reading. If you are uncertain, administer the screening tests found in this book.

▶ **Understand What Your Child Needs.** Learn your child's strengths and weaknesses as well as his or her academic needs. This information will come from an independent diagnostic evaluation. It is important that you understand what is in that report.

▶ **Learn About the Reading Process.** Why do children have trouble with reading and what can be done to help them? Learn about the key elements of good evidence-based reading instruction.

▶ **Know Your Rights.** IDEA 2004 provides you and your child with educational rights. There are good resources for learning about this.

▶ **Advocate for Your Child.** Build your team, get organized, network with other parents, and learn to interact effectively with your school system. Find your voice.

---

you are not alone. There are those in your local community who know the ropes: mothers who have fought to find the best teachers for their children, fathers who have taken the time to attend team meetings, and families who have successfully garnered the services that have resulted in reading gains for their sons and daughters. Make it your mission to find these people. They are your key not only to knowledge about your local area but also to emotional support as you navigate the system.

FINAL TIPS

You are almost ready to begin your journey! Here are a few last tips.

▶ **Ask, Ask, Ask!** Don't hesitate to ask questions—of anyone and everyone who might be able to help you along the way. Who are the other families with children who are also struggling to read? What have they tried? Which school systems provide the best services? Is school choice an option in your community? Who are the strongest educational advocates in your area? Which professionally trained tutors are getting results?

▶ **Read everything you can.** Look for "mainstream" material. Often, as parents, we are vulnerable to every "quick fix" appearing in the media. We desperately want to help our children; we will sacrifice whatever we must. Unfortunately, our great concern for our children makes us easy prey for entrepreneurs and sincere, but mistaken, individuals who promise simple solutions. Instead of looking for a quick answer, look for top professionals in the field. Read the materials endorsed by the *International Dyslexia Association*, *Learning Disabilities Association*, and *National Center for Learning Disabilities*. Find out about the most effective, research-based methods that have been getting results for years.

▶ **Make use of all resources.** In your search to understand, be aware that there are many organizations that can help. Tap into local, state, and federal agencies as well as national and private organizations.

▶ **Trust your own impressions.** Research has shown that a mother's instinct kicks in before teachers and other professionals even realize there is a problem. Don't second-guess yourself. There may be days when you get discouraged and times when you are made to believe that all of this is just in your head. Press on. If something doesn't seem right, don't silence your own misgivings. Ask questions. Explore what is bothering you. Keep looking for answers.

▶ **Never give up hope.** While it is crucial to face the fact that your child is not going to learn in the way that others do, it is equally as important to believe in your child. When the entire world has written her off, when nobody is on her side, you must be the one to still believe. You must press on, knowing that the person for whom you are advocating is infinitely worth it.

▶ **Talk to your child.** Let your child know you support her. Reassure her that you realize she is working hard and you understand that her struggle to read is not her fault. Without a doubt, your child is keenly aware of the trouble she is having and will find it helpful to talk about it. Include her in the journey when appropriate. It is important that children understand why they are having trouble and what they need to enable them to become successful readers. Eventually, they must learn to advocate for themselves, and, like you, they will need an understanding of their strengths and weaknesses. This is a gradual process for children, and the level of their involvement is dependent on what is appropriate for their age. Adolescents require a sense of control of what is happening to them that is not appropriate for a younger child. It is important to note, however, that it is not wise to include children in the struggle between parents and school systems. You do not want to undermine a child's confidence in teachers or in education in general.

▶ **Find positive role models.** There are many people with dyslexia who have made significant contributions to society. It is important for you and your child to focus on those who have stayed the course and found their niche. Steven Spielberg, the noted director of such movies as *E.T. the Extra-Terrestrial, Jaws, Schindler's List, The Color Purple,* and *Raiders of the Lost Ark,* discovered in adulthood that there was a name for the struggle that plagued his school years. Diagnosed as a dyslexic, he recently shed some light on the reason for his renowned success, despite the lack of awareness of learning disabilities in the 1950s. He acknowledged the impact of his parents, who helped him endlessly with his studies. They provided the support he needed to make sure he did as well as he possibly could in school. [33]

It has been said that a child who wants to learn and can't is part of the world gone wrong. As an involved parent who has taken the time to read this book, you are about to set the world right. You will encounter those who will call you an overinvolved parent. Stay the course. Your child's whole future depends on it.

---

33   Retrieved from http://www.ldresources.org/2012/09/steven-spielberg-discusses-his-dyslexia-with-quinn-bradlee/

GLOSSARY OF TERMS

Accommodations (educational): Support services students receive to do grade-level work, such as listening to stories read on the computer. Accommodations do not substantially change the instructional level, the content of instruction, or the performance criteria.

Age-equivalent scores: Standardized scores that are equivalent to the average score for students at that age level.

Attention-deficit/hyperactivity disorder (ADHD): A persistent pattern of inattention and/or hyperactivity-impulsivity that interferes with functioning or development. Several symptoms need to be present in more than one setting to qualify for a diagnosis. ADHD is not a learning disability, although some children may have ADHD as well as a reading disability.

Auditory processing disorder: A neurological disorder that results in difficulty perceiving and understanding oral language despite having good hearing acuity. There are several types of auditory processing disorders that affect how auditory information is interpreted or processed by the brain. The diagnosis must be made by an audiologist in a sound-treated room.

Cognitive functioning: The ability to process thoughts and attain information. Cognitive functions include language, memory, attention and all aspects of perception, thinking and reasoning.

Common Core State Standards: Academic standards in math and English language arts/literacy (ELA) that outline what every student should know and be able to do from kindergarten through 12th grade.

Composite or cluster score: A score that results from combining individual test scores. Composite scores can be misleading when the scores on individual tests within the cluster are not similar.

Consonant blends: Two or more consonants grouped together, in which each consonant makes a *separate* sound, thus producing two or more distinct sounds. For example, the letters *st* in the word *stop* are a consonant blend.

Consonant digraphs: Two consonants that are grouped together to make *one* sound. For example, the letters *ch* in the word *chop* are a consonant digraph.

Criterion-referenced tests: Informal measures of what a child can do based on the acquisition of specific information and skills. For example, a student may be tested on his knowledge of multiplication facts or letter names.

Decoding: The ability to translate print into speech by rapidly recognizing and analyzing printed words. This involves matching letters or letter combinations to their sounds and recognizing the patterns that make syllables and words.

Diagnostic evaluation: A comprehensive assessment of a child given by a professional certified in the field of education or psychology.

Dyscalculia: A math disability in which a student has difficulty with numbers and number concepts, learning math facts and solving math problems.

Dysgraphia: Difficulty with writing that requires a complex set of motor and information processing skills.

Dyslexia: A language-based learning disability that interferes with reading and other language-based skills, such as spelling and writing. This is the most common type of learning disability and may also be referred to as a reading disability. Dyslexia is neurologically based and is not due to an impoverished environment or to poor instruction.

Encoding: The ability to spell or convert spoken words into written form, translating individual sounds into letters. When we spell, or encode, we put something into a code. When we read, or decode, we take words out of a code. Thus, spelling and reading are opposites.

Executive functioning: Mental processes that are coordinated in the brain's frontal lobe and enable an individual to plan, organize, carry out and monitor purposeful cognitive activity. This involves attention, working memory, reasoning and cognitive flexibility.

FAPE: An acronym that refers to a "free, appropriate public education" guaranteed by the federal special education law, IDEA 2004, to all children with disabilities between the ages of 3 and 21.

Grade-equivalent score: A standardized score that is equivalent to the average score for students at that grade level.

IDEA 2004: A federal special education law that applies to all states and to all public schools that guarantees to every child a free, appropriate public education in the least restrictive environment. The federal regulations that accompany the law add to and explain the law. Individual states have also each enacted their own state laws and regulations. Although individual states may exceed the standards set forth in the federal law, all states must *at least* meet the requirements of IDEA 2004.

Individual education program (IEP): A document that outlines the amount of help and the type of services a child will receive in special education under the federal special education law IDEA 2004.

Intellectual ability: An individual's ability to think, problem-solve, and understand ideas and information.

Learning disability: A neurological disorder caused by differences in brain structure or functioning that interferes with the ability to process, store, or produce information and that can affect the ability to read, write, speak or do math.

Mean score: The *average* score obtained by students of similar ages and grades taking the same standardized test.

Modifications (educational): Changes that alter the content, instructional level or performance criteria of the curriculum, such as providing third grade spelling words for a fifth grade student.

No Child Left Behind (The Elementary and Secondary Education Act) (NCLB): A law that sets clear regulations for students who receive reading help under special education, requiring schools to provide instruction in evidence-based methods of reading.

Nonverbal learning disability (NVLD): A learning disability characterized by strong verbal skills contrasted by lower nonverbal skills. Individuals may be very verbal and decode well, but have trouble interpreting what they read, interacting socially, making sense of information, putting together the parts to see the whole, and perceiving how things interact in physical space. The disability tends to progress with age, and many individuals with NVLD develop problems with anxiety and depression.

Nonverbal reasoning: Reasoning and problem-solving that does not involve verbal language ability. Tests of nonverbal reasoning are generally based on shapes, pictures, and diagrams and evaluate logical thinking.

Normal distribution: A description of the bell-shaped curve that scores form on a graph, indicating that most scores cluster in the middle, average area. Remaining scores taper off evenly on either side (high and low).

Orthographic processing: The ability to form, store and access the visual look of a word or string of letters.

Parent advisory committee (PAC): A school-based parent group that provides support and information to parents whose children are involved in special education.

Percentile rank: A standardized test ranking that indicates the percentage of test takers scoring at or below the student's standard score.

Phoneme: The smallest unit of sound in a language that has meaning. For example, the sound of a single letter (*t*) is a phoneme.

Phonemic awareness: The ability to identify and manipulate individual sounds in a word.

Phonics: The association of sounds with letters.

Phonological awareness: A broad skill that includes the ability to identify and manipulate units of oral language, such as parts of words, syllables, and onset rimes.

Processing speed: The ability to process overlearned and relatively easy cognitive information automatically and swiftly without intentional thinking; a measure of cognitive efficiency.

Progress monitoring: Informal assessments used to evaluate a student's ongoing academic progress and to evaluate the effectiveness of instruction.

Raw score: Total number of correct answers on a test.

Reading comprehension: The ability to understand what is read, including explicit and inferential information in a passage.

Reading disability: A broad term used by many professionals that refers to all students who struggle with reading. This includes all children on the continuum of severity of reading problems, ranging from those with mild reading problems to those with the most severe reading problems. It includes those with dyslexia.

Reading fluency: The ability to read words accurately and automatically.

Remediate: To correct or improve a deficiency or problem. *Reading remediation* refers to the act of remedying or reversing a reading problem.

Response to intervention (RTI): A tiered educational program designed to identify struggling students early and provide appropriate instruction, thus preventing the need to refer a child for special education.

Special education advocate: A specialist trained in special education law with considerable experience working with school systems. While advocates are not usually lawyers, they have expertise in the area.

Special education attorney: An attorney who specializes in special education law.

Specific learning disability: A disorder in one or more of the basic cognitive processes involved in understanding or in using spoken or written language that may manifest itself in the imperfect ability to listen, think, speak, read, write, spell, or do math calculations. It includes dyslexia.

Standard deviation: A standardized measure that describes how much higher or lower a standardized test score lies compared to the mean (average score). In education and psychology, if the mean standard score of a test is 10, then the standard deviation is 3. If the mean standard score of a test is 100, then the standard deviation is 15.

Standardized tests: Tests that compare the test taker's performance with the scores of other students across the country who are at the same age or grade-level. Sometimes called "norm-referenced tests," these test results are often expressed in standard scores and percentile ranking.

Structured literacy: Explicit and systematic reading instruction that includes the following elements: phonology, sound-symbol association, syllable instruction, morphology, syntax, and semantics.

Title I educational programs: Federally funded programs provided to schools in economically designated areas for students in need of help in reading and math.

Visual processing disorder: A hindered ability to make sense of information taken in through the eyes despite good visual acuity, affecting the manner in which visual information is interpreted or processed by the brain.

Vowel digraphs: Two vowels that, when grouped together, make a single sound. For example, the letters *ea* in the word *each* are a vowel digraph.

Whole language: A method of teaching reading and writing that emphasizes learning whole words and phrases by encountering them in meaningful contexts rather than by phonics exercises.

APPENDIX A

Informal Screening for Children at the End of Kindergarten

Copyright 2015 Lorna Kaufman

The informal screening tests were developed to help parents determine whether or not their child needs help with reading and whether or not they should seek a professional, independent evaluation. These screening tests should not take the place of a professional evaluation. The **sole** purpose of the screening documents is to help parents decide whether or not they need to take the next step and have their child evaluated by a qualified professional.

By using the screening documents the reader acknowledges that he or she will only use them for the purpose described above—as a tool in their decision-making process to help decide whether or not to consult a professional independent evaluator with regard to their child's reading ability.

The screening documents should **never** be used for the following:

- ▶ To monitor a student's reading progress
- ▶ To determine a student's reading skills
- ▶ For purposes of an IEP
- ▶ For purposes of diagnosis

INSTRUCTIONS FOR ADMINISTERING SCREENING TESTS:

Visit www.SmartKidCantRead.com to download full-sized (ready-to-use) copies of both parent and child versions of these tests. The website has videos where you can see these tests administered.

a. This screening test is designed to be administered to children who are near the end of their kindergarten year.

b. You can administer the kindergarten test in two sessions if you prefer.

c. You will need the following materials:

    i. Testing Guidelines

    ii. Parent Test Materials

        1. Kindergarten Informal Screening Test (6 pages)

        2. Parent Scoring Sheets (3 pages)

    iii. Child Test Materials

        1. Kindergarten Child Letter and Sound Identification Page

        2. A piece of lined paper and a pencil for your child to use.

TESTING GUIDELINES

- ▶ Choose a time when your child is not tired or distracted. Keep in mind that children are often tired after school.

- ▶ Choose a quiet, well-lit room where you will not be interrupted.

- ▶ Sit at a table adjacent to your child (see video).

- ▶ If your child asks you for help, first ask him what he thinks the answer is. If he is unable to respond, you can either tell him the answer or move along in a reassuring way. This counts as an error.

- ▶ If your child does not know an answer, don't wait too long. Just ask him if he wants to skip that one and move on to the next.

- ▶ Don't correct your child if he makes an error.

- ▶ Be encouraging to your child, no matter how many words he reads incorrectly.

- ▶ Use the Parent Scoring Sheet to record your child's answers on all tests.

- ▶ Have your child leave the room before you score the test.

- ▶ If you find that your child has difficulty with the tests, *stop the testing*. Please do not become impatient with your child. Remember, he is doing the best he can. You have taken the first step, and now it is time for you to take the next one.

KINDERGARTEN INFORMAL SCREENING TEST (PAGE 1)

Letter and Sound Identification Subtest

1. Give your child a piece of lined paper and ask him to *write his first and last name*. (*Most children can write their names.*)

2. Using lined paper, *dictate the following letters* for your child to write. Your child may choose to write either a capital or small letter. Both are acceptable.

    (*Most children can write most—but not all—letters. Some letter reversals are normal at this age and do not count as errors.*)

    # A, F, T, B, G, H, C, D, M, O, J, K, I,
    # L, P, Q, E, W, Z, N, R, U, S, V, X, Y

3. Using the Kindergarten Letter and Sound Identification Page, point to one letter at a time and ask your child to *name each letter*. (*Most children can name most of the letters.*)

4. Using the Kindergarten Letter and Sound Identification Page, point to one letter at a time and ask your child to tell you the *sound for each letter*.

    See the kindergarten video at *www.SmartKidCantRead.com* for a demonstration of the correct vowel sounds.

    (*Most children can give the sounds for most letters, although vowels are more difficult than consonants and may not be mastered by the end of kindergarten.*)

KINDERGARTEN INFORMAL SCREENING TEST (PAGE 2)

Kindergarten Rhyme and Initial Sound Subtest

1. **Identify rhymes.** Tell your child you are going to read some words, and ask him to tell you if the words rhyme.

    (*Most children will be able to identify all rhymes.*)

    Do an example together so that he can see what is expected: Sat and cat rhyme; they both sound the same at the end. Bit and fit rhyme. They both have the same sound at the end.

    - Do *sit* and *hit* rhyme? (*yes*)

    - Do *man* and *dog* rhyme? (*no*)

    - Do *car* and *star* rhyme? (*yes*)

    - Do *mat* and *mud* rhyme? (*no*)

    - Do *can* and *cat* rhyme? (*no*)

    - Do *book* and *look* rhyme? (*yes*)

KINDERGARTEN INFORMAL SCREENING TEST (PAGE 3)

2. **Produce rhymes.** It is more difficult to think of a rhyming word than it is to determine whether two given words rhyme.

   (*Most children will be able to produce one rhyming word for each target word.*)

   - In this exercise, tell your child you are going to play a game with rhyming words. You will say a word, and you want him to repeat the word.

     If your child says the word incorrectly, pronounce the word again slowly and ask him to repeat so that he is able to say the word clearly.

   - Next, ask him to tell you a word that rhymes with the word he just repeated.

     Do the first word (tree) together so that he understands what is expected.

   - Parent: "Say tree." (Wait for your child to repeat the word.)
     Parent: "Can you tell me a word that rhymes with 'tree'?"
     (*me, bee, he, she, see, knee, tea, etc.*)

   - Parent: "Say make." (Wait for your child to repeat the word.)
     Parent: "Can you tell me a word that rhymes with 'make'?"
     (*lake, take, shake, break, etc.*)

   - Parent: "Say cat." (Wait for your child to repeat the word.)
     Parent: "Can you tell me a word that rhymes with 'cat'?"
     (*hat, bat, sat, rat, chat, that, etc.*)

   - Parent: "Say star." (Wait for your child to repeat the word.)
     Parent: "Can you tell me a word that rhymes with 'star'?"
     (*car, jar, far, tar, bar, etc.*)

   - Parent: "Say rug." (Wait for your child to repeat the word.)
     Parent: "Can you tell me a word that rhymes with 'rug'?"
     (*hug, mug, bug, dug, jug, tug, etc.*)

KINDERGARTEN INFORMAL SCREENING TEST (PAGE 4)

- Parent: "Say kick." (Wait for your child to repeat the word.)
Parent: "Can you tell me a word that rhymes with 'kick'?"
(*lick, pick, sick, click, tick, etc.*)

KINDERGARTEN INFORMAL SCREENING TEST (PAGE 5)

3. **Identify initial sounds in words.** Make sure that you have your
   child identify the initial sound and not the letter.
   (*Children should be able to identify most of the initial sounds.*)

   - In this exercise, tell your child you are going to play a game with
     words. You will say a word, and you want him to repeat the word.
     *If he repeats the word incorrectly, say it again slowly and ask
     him to repeat so that he says the word clearly.*

   - Next, ask him to make the beginning sound of the word he
     just repeated.
     (Note that when a letter appears in brackets—for example, /h/—it
     refers to the *sound* of the letter and not the name of the letter.)
     Do the first word (moon) together by telling him that the
     first sound in moon is /m/.
     (*Most children will be able to identify these initial sounds with
     only one error.*)

   - Parent: "Say moon." (Wait for your child to say moon.)
     Parent: "What is the first sound in moon?" */m/*

   - Parent: "Say cake." (Wait for your child to say cake.)
     Parent: "What is the first sound in cake?" */k/*

   - Parent: "Say boat." (Wait for your child to say boat.)
     Parent: "What is the first sound in boat?" */b/*

   - Parent: "Say table." (Wait for your child to say table.)
     Parent: "What is the first sound in table?" */t/*

   - Parent: "Say light." (Wait for your child to say light.)
     Parent: "What is the first sound in light?" */l/*

   - Parent: "Say sing." (Wait for your child to say sing.)
     Parent: "What is the first sound in sing?" */s/*

KINDERGARTEN INFORMAL SCREENING TEST (PAGE 6)

Kindergarten Listening Comprehension Subtest

Read the following story to your child. After you have finished reading, ask him to tell you about the story and explain what happened.

Introduce the story by telling your child that you are going to read a story called "The Best Birthday Present." Ask your child to tell you about his best birthday present.

The Best Birthday Present

Last week was Judy's sixth birthday. Mom and Dad gave her a birthday party. Some of her friends from kindergarten came to her house. They had ice cream and cake. They had lots of fun and went outside to play.

Judy opened her presents after they came back inside. Her mom and dad gave her a doll, and she got books and games from her friends.

Judy's grandparents got to the party late. They gave Judy a big hug and told her to come out to the car to see her birthday present. Sitting on the back seat of the car was the best present of all—a little ball of black fur—a new kitten!

QUESTIONS

1. Ask your child to retell the story in his own words. Does he tell it in a logical sequence? Does he recall the main points?
2. Who was having a birthday party? (*Judy*)
3. What did they do at the party? (*Any of these is correct: ate ice cream and cake; played outside; opened presents*)
4. Who gave her the best present? (*Her grandparents*)
5. What was the best present? (*A little black kitten*)

CHILD PAGE

Kindergarten Letter and Sound Identification Page

Name

A	D	P	R
F	M	Q	U
T	O	E	S
B	J	W	V
G	K	Z	X
H	I	N	Y
C	L		

PARENT SCORING SHEET (PAGE 1)

Mark correct answers with a checkmark ✓. Mark incorrect answers with a dash ▬.

    1a. _____First name

    1b. _____Last name

2. Written letters

_____A	_____D	_____P	_____R
_____F	_____M	_____Q	_____U
_____T	_____O	_____E	_____S
_____B	_____J	_____W	_____V
_____G	_____K	_____Z	_____X
_____H	_____I	_____N	_____Y
_____C	_____L		

3. Names of letters

_____A	_____D	_____P	_____R
_____F	_____M	_____Q	_____U
_____T	_____O	_____E	_____S
_____B	_____J	_____W	_____V
_____G	_____K	_____Z	_____X
_____H	_____I	_____N	_____Y
_____C	_____L		

PARENT SCORING SHEET (PAGE 2)

4. Sounds of letters

_____A   _____D   _____P   _____R

_____F   _____M   _____Q   _____U

_____T   _____O   _____E   _____S

_____B   _____J   _____W   _____V

_____G   _____K   _____Z   _____X

_____H   _____I   _____N   _____Y

_____C   _____L

5. Recognizing rhyming words

_____Sit/Hit (yes)   _____Mat/Mud (no)

_____Man/Dog (no)   _____Can/Cat (no)

_____Car/Star (yes)   _____Book/Look (yes)

6. Producing rhyming words

_____Tree   _____Star

_____Make   _____Rug

_____Cat   _____Kick

7. Identifying initial sounds

_____Moon /m/   _____Table /t/

_____Cake /k/   _____Light /l/

_____Boat /b/   _____Sing /s/

PARENT SCORING SHEET (PAGE 3)

8. Listening Comprehension

Story Retell (details in logical order):

_____Birthday party

_____Friends came

_____Had fun (include at least one: ice cream and cake, played outside, opened presents)

_____Grandparents came (new kitten)

Questions

_____Who was having the party? (Judy)

_____What did they do at the party? (Include at least one: ate ice cream and cake, played outside, opened presents)

_____Who gave her the best present? (Her grandparents)

_____What was the best present? (A little black kitten)

APPENDIX B

Informal Screening for Children at the End of First Grade

Copyright 2015 Lorna Kaufman

The informal screening tests were developed to help parents determine whether or not their child needs help with reading and whether or not they should seek a professional, independent evaluation. These screening tests should not take the place of a professional evaluation. The **sole** purpose of the screening documents is to help parents decide whether or not they need to take the next step and have their child evaluated by a qualified professional.

By using the screening documents the reader acknowledges that he or she will only use them for the purpose described above—as a tool in their decision-making process to help decide whether or not to consult a professional independent evaluator with regard to their child's reading ability.

The screening documents should **never** be used for the following:

- ▶ To monitor a student's reading progress
- ▶ To determine a student's reading skills
- ▶ For purposes of an IEP
- ▶ For purposes of diagnosis

These documents are intended only for the use of the individual reader and duplication or distribution is prohibited.

INSTRUCTIONS FOR ADMINISTERING SCREENING TESTS

Visit www.SmartKidCantRead.com to download full-sized (ready-to-use) copies of both parent and child versions of these tests. The website has videos where you can see these tests administered.

1. You will notice that there are two copies of the first-grade word lists and passages. One copy is for your use, and one is for your child.

2. The First Grade Informal Screening test is intended to be administered to children at the end of their first grade year. The word lists and passages represent skills that children should have by the end of the year.

3. If you find that your child has difficulty with the tests, *stop the testing*. Please do not become impatient with your child. Remember, he is doing the best he can. You have taken the first step, and now it is time for you to take the next one.

4. The First Grade Informal Screening Test includes:

   i. Testing Guidelines
   ii. Parent Testing Materials:
       1. Word Recognition List
       2. Two Reading Passages
   iii. Child Testing Materials:
       1. Word Recognition List
       2. Two Reading Passages

TESTING GUIDELINES

▶ Choose a time when your child is not tired or distracted. Keep in mind that children are often tired after school.

▶ Choose a quiet, well-lit room where you will not be interrupted.

▶ Sit at a table adjacent to your child (see video).

▶ If your child asks you what a word is, first ask if he can sound it out. If he cannot, you can either tell him the word or move along. This counts as an error.

▶ If your child does not respond to a word, ask him if he can read the word. If not, say, "Let's try the next one." This counts as an error.

▶ Don't correct your child if he makes an error.

▶ Be encouraging to your child, no matter how many words he reads incorrectly.

▶ Have your child leave the room before you score the test.

▶ **Word list reading:** Place a check mark next to each word he reads correctly and a dash next to each incorrectly read word. It is important to make some type of mark beside each word so that your child does not know when you are marking incorrect responses.

▶ **Passage reading:** Each of the following counts as one error.

  • **Mark a line through each word read incorrectly.** This includes any word that the student pronounces correctly, but omits the ending. For example, if the word is "runs" and the child reads "run," mark a line through the word: ~~run~~.

- **Circle** each word that the child *leaves out.*
- **Place a caret** (⋀) where extra words are *inserted.*

▶ Excessive self-corrections and repetitions, while not scored here, can be indicative of problems with decoding. Do not worry about marking self-corrections and repeated words and phrases now, but be aware of their significance.

INFORMAL SCREENING FOR CHILDREN AT THE END OF FIRST GRADE

Parent Page: Grade 1 Word List 101

Ask your child to read the following list of words.

(A child at the end of the first grade should be able to read this list of words without hesitation and miss no more than three words.)

Mark correct answers with a checkmark ✓. Mark incorrect answers with a dash —.

sat	then
hit	stay
to	is
map	saw
you	some
chin	boat
shop	happy
cat	pail
home	as
like	trim
stop	father
when	ask
shape	had
help	take
of	pit
let	

CHILD PAGE: WORD LIST 101

sat	then
hit	stay
to	is
map	saw
you	some
chin	boat
shop	happy
cat	pail
home	as
like	trim
stop	father
when	ask
shape	had
help	take
of	pit
let	

PARENT PAGE: GRADE 1 PASSAGE 101

Ask your child to read the following two passages *out loud*. Tell him you will ask him some questions after he finishes the story. These are passages appropriate for a reader at the end of first grade. The first passage is somewhat easier than the second passage.

(*A first-grade student should be able to read the first passage with no more than 1–2 errors. He should be able to read at a normal rate without stumbling over words. He should be able to answer all of the questions at the end of the passage.*)

Introduce this story by telling your child that it is about a cat named Tom.

Tom

I have a white cat. His name is Tom. Tom likes to sit in the sun. He likes to sleep on the rug in the sun. The rug is by the door. We try not to step on him when we open the door. Tom likes to play with my red ball. He runs for the ball.

Read the following questions to your child after he finishes reading the story.

1. What is the name of the cat? (*Tom*)

2. What does the cat like to do? (*Any of these is correct: sleep on the rug; sleep in the sun; play with the red ball*)

3. Where does the cat like to sleep? (*Any of these is correct: on the rug; in front of the door; in the sun*)

CHILD PAGE: PASSAGE 101

Tom

I have a white cat. His name is Tom. Tom likes to sit in the sun. He likes to sleep on the rug in the sun. The rug is by the door. We try not to step on him when we open the door. Tom likes to play with my red ball. He runs for the ball.

PARENT PAGE: GRADE 1 PASSAGE 102

A student who is completing the first grade should be able to read this second passage with no more than 2–3 errors. He should be able to read the passage at a normal rate without stumbling over words or stopping to sound out words. Students should be able to answer the questions at the end of the passage.

Introduce this story by telling your child that it is a story about a boy and his dog.

Jake and His Dog

Jake went for a walk with his dog. His dog's name was Mugs. Jake and Mugs ran into the woods by his house. They ran on the path to the lake. Jake did not go in the water but he got his feet wet. He threw sticks into the water and Mugs ran in after them.

Read the following questions to your child after he finishes reading the story.

1. Where did Jake go? (*Any of these is correct: to the lake; for a walk; into the woods*)

2. Who went with Jake? (*Mugs, or his dog*)

3. What did Jake do? (*Any of these is correct: he threw sticks in the water; he got his feet wet; he went for a walk; he went to the lake*)

CHILD PAGE: PASSAGE 102

Jake and His Dog

Jake went for a walk with his dog. His dog's name was Mugs. Jake and Mugs ran into the woods by his house. They ran on the path to the lake. Jake did not go in the water but he got his feet wet. He threw sticks into the water and Mugs ran in after them.

APPENDIX C

Informal Screening for Children at the End of Second Grade

The informal screening tests were developed to help parents determine whether or not their child needs help with reading and whether or not they should seek a professional, independent evaluation. These screening tests should not take the place of a professional evaluation. The **sole** purpose of the screening documents is to help parents decide whether or not they need to take the next step and have their child evaluated by a qualified professional.

By using the screening documents the reader acknowledges that he or she will only use them for the purpose described above—as a tool in their decision-making process to help decide whether or not to consult a professional independent evaluator with regard to their child's reading ability.

The screening documents should **never** be used for the following:

- ▶ To monitor a student's reading progress
- ▶ To determine a student's reading skills
- ▶ For purposes of an IEP
- ▶ For purposes of diagnosis

INSTRUCTIONS FOR ADMINISTERING SCREENING TESTS

Visit www.SmartKidCantRead.com to download full-sized (ready-to-use) copies of both parent and child versions of these tests. The website has videos where you can see these tests administered.

1. You will notice that there are two copies of the second grade word lists and passages. One copy is for your use, and one is for your child.

2. The Second Grade Screening test is intended to be administered to children at the end of their second-grade year. The word lists and passages represent skills that children should have by the end of the year.

3. If you find that your child has difficulty with the tests, *stop the testing.* Please do not become impatient with your child. Remember, he is doing the best he can. You have taken the first step, and now it is time for you to take the next one.

4. The Second Grade Informal Screening Test packet includes:

   i.   Testing Guidelines
   ii. Parent Testing Materials:
        1. Word Recognition List
        2. Two Reading Passages
   iii. Child Testing Materials:
        1. Word Recognition List
        2. Two Reading Passages

TESTING GUIDELINES

- ▶ Choose a time when your child is not tired or distracted. Keep in mind that children are often tired after school.

- ▶ Choose a quiet, well-lit room where you will not be interrupted.

- ▶ Sit at a table adjacent to your child (see video).

- ▶ If your child asks you what a word is, first ask if he can sound it out. If he cannot, tell him the word. This counts as an error.

- ▶ If your child does not respond to a word, ask him if he can read the word. If not, say, "Let's try the next one." This counts as an error.

- ▶ Don't correct your child if he makes an error.

- ▶ Be encouraging to your child, no matter how many words he reads incorrectly.

- ▶ Have your child leave the room before you score the test.

- ▶ **Word list reading:** Place a check mark next to each word he reads correctly and a dash next to each incorrectly read word. It is important to make some type of mark beside each word so that your child does not know when you are marking incorrect words.

- ▶ **Passage reading:** Each of the following counts as one error.

  - • **Mark a line through each word read incorrectly.** This includes any word that the student pronounces correctly, but omits the ending for. For example, if the word is "ran" and the child reads "runs," mark a line through the word: ~~ran.~~

  - • **Circle** each word that the child *leaves out.*

- **Place a caret** ($\wedge$) where extra words are *inserted*.

▶ Excessive self-corrections and repetitions, while not scored here, can be indicative of problems with decoding. Do not worry about marking self-corrections and repeated words and phrases now, but be aware of their significance.

PARENT PAGE: GRADE 2 WORD LIST 201

Ask your child to read the following list of words out loud. A child who is *completing* the second grade should be able to read the words accurately and without hesitation and miss no more than three words.

Mark correct answers with a checkmark ✓. Mark incorrect answers with a dash ▬.

meat	found
bring	before
sudden	pancake
listen	footstep
because	muffin
stopping	ladder
waited	mistake
grapes	sunshine
lifted	invite
does	fishing
write	your
napkin	hurry
chicken	drink
very	always
snow	around

CHILD PAGE: WORD LIST 201

meat	found
bring	before
sudden	pancake
listen	footstep
because	muffin
stopping	ladder
waited	mistake
grapes	sunshine
lifted	invite
does	fishing
write	your
napkin	hurry
chicken	drink
very	always
snow	around

PARENT PAGE: GRADE 2 PASSAGE 201

Ask your child to read the following two passages **out loud** and answer the questions at the end of each passage.

Introduce this passage by telling your child that it is about a birthday surprise.

Mother's Birthday

My sister and I picked flowers for Mother's birthday. We picked the red roses from the garden in our back yard. We took the flowers into the house and put them in a vase of water. Then we baked a white cake. We put pink frosting on the cake. Mother was surprised to see the flowers and cake. She was very happy and gave us both a big hug and kiss.

Read the following questions to your child after he finishes reading the story.

1. Who was having a birthday? (*Mother*)

2. What did the children do? (*Any of these is correct: picked flowers from the garden; put flowers in a vase of water; baked a cake*)

3. How did Mother feel? (*Happy or surprised*)

CHILD PAGE: PASSAGE 201

Mother's Birthday

My sister and I picked flowers for Mother's birthday. We picked the red roses from the garden in our back yard. We took the flowers into the house and put them in a vase of water. Then we baked a white cake. We put pink frosting on the cake. Mother was surprised to see the flowers and cake. She was very happy and gave us both a big hug and kiss.

PARENT PAGE: GRADE 2 PASSAGE 202

Introduce this passage by telling your child that it is about finding a lost puppy.

The Lost Puppy

Dad and I went to the park to play basketball. A cute puppy came to play with us. He was black with a pink nose. He jumped on me and licked my face. I think he was lost. I asked my dad if we could keep him. Dad said we had to find his owners because they would want him back. We called the police and they came to pick him up. They said they would try to find his owners. I was very sad.

Read the following questions to your child after he finishes reading the story.

1. What did they find in the park? (*A puppy*)

2. What did the puppy look like? (*Cute; black with a pink nose*)

3. What did his father say they had to do? (*Find the owners or call the police*)

4. Why was the boy sad? (*Because he would miss the dog; he wanted to keep the dog*)

CHILD PAGE: PASSAGE 202

The Lost Puppy

Dad and I went to the park to play basketball. A cute puppy came to play with us. He was black with a pink nose. He jumped on me and licked my face. I think he was lost. I asked my dad if we could keep him. Dad said we had to find his owners because they would want him back. We called the police and they came to pick him up. They said they would try to find his owners. I was very sad.

APPENDIX D

Informal Screening for Children at the End of Third Grade

The informal screening tests were developed to help parents determine whether or not their child needs help with reading and whether or not they should seek a professional, independent evaluation. These screening tests should not take the place of a professional evaluation. The **sole** purpose of the screening documents is to help parents decide whether or not they need to take the next step and have their child evaluated by a qualified professional.

By using the screening documents the reader acknowledges that he or she will only use them for the purpose described above—as a tool in their decision-making process to help decide whether or not to consult a professional independent evaluator with regard to their child's reading ability.

The screening documents should **never** be used for the following:

- ▶ To monitor a student's reading progress
- ▶ To determine a student's reading skills
- ▶ For purposes of an IEP
- ▶ For purposes of diagnosis

INSTRUCTIONS FOR ADMINISTERING SCREENING TESTS

Visit www.SmartKidCantRead.com to download full-sized (ready-to-use) copies of both parent and child versions of these tests. The website has videos where you can see these tests administered.

1. You will notice that there are two copies of the third-grade word lists and passages. One copy is for your use, and one is for your child.

2. The Third Grade Screening test is intended to be administered to children at the end of their third-grade year. The word lists and passages represent skills that children should have by the end of the year.

3. If you find that your child has difficulty with the tests, *stop the testing.* Please do not become impatient with your child. Remember, he is doing the best he can. You have taken the first step, and now it is time for you to take the next one.

4. The Third Grade Informal Screening Test packet includes:

   i.   Testing Guidelines
   ii. Parent Testing Materials:
        1. Word Recognition List
        2. Two Reading Passages
   iii. Child Testing Materials:
        1. Word Recognition List
        2. Two Reading Passages

TESTING GUIDELINES

- ▶ Choose a time when your child is not tired or distracted. Keep in mind that children are often tired after school.

- ▶ Choose a quiet, well-lit room where you will not be interrupted.

- ▶ Sit at a table adjacent to your child (see video).

- ▶ If your child asks you what a word is, first ask if he can sound it out. If he cannot, tell him the word. This counts as an error.

- ▶ If your child does not respond to a word, ask him if he can read the word. If not, say, "Let's try the next one." This counts as an error.

- ▶ Don't correct your child if he makes an error.

- ▶ Be encouraging to your child, no matter how many words he reads incorrectly.

- ▶ Have your child leave the room before you score the test.

- ▶ **Word list reading:** Place a check mark next to each word he reads correctly and a dash next to each incorrectly read word. It is important to make some type of mark beside each word so that your child does not know when you are marking incorrect words.

- ▶ **Passage reading:** Each of the following counts as one error.

  - • **Mark a line through each word read incorrectly.** This includes any word that the student pronounces correctly, but omits the ending for. For example, if the word is "ran" and the child reads "runs," mark a line through the word: ~~ran~~.

  - • **Circle** each word that the child *leaves out*.

Place a caret (∧) where extra words are *inserted*.

▶ Excessive self-corrections and repetitions, while not scored here, can be indicative of problems with decoding. Do not worry about marking self-corrections and repeated words and phrases now, but be aware of their significance.

PARENT PAGE: GRADE 3 WORD LIST 301

Ask your child to read the following list of words out loud. A student who is *completing* the third grade should be able to read these words with accuracy and fluency and miss no more than three words.

Mark correct answers with a checkmark ✓. Mark incorrect answers with a dash —.

word	draw
which	written
about	cleaned
drinking	myself
together	treasure
impossible	station
starting	stream
sounds	building
between	warmer
never	silence
decide	quickly
understand	should
more	

CHILD PAGE: WORD LIST 301

word

which

about

drinking

together

impossible

starting

sounds

between

never

decide

understand

more

draw

written

cleaned

myself

treasure

station

stream

building

warmer

silence

quickly

should

PARENT PAGE: GRADE 3 PASSAGE 301

Ask your child to the read the following two passages **out loud**. A child who is *completing* the third grade should be able to read the passages fluently with no more than 2–3 errors.

Introduce this passage by telling your child that it is about learning to play chess.

Playing Chess

Last year Jason's mother took him to the library where children were playing chess in an after-school club. Jason thought it looked like fun. He decided he wanted to join the chess program. At first he was very afraid because most of the kids were older. He was afraid the other boys would laugh at him because he did not know how to play. But they were really nice to him and showed him how to play. Jason soon became an expert at chess. Tomorrow is Jason's big day: He is entering his first chess tournament! Good luck, Jason!

Read the following questions to your child after he finishes reading the story.

1. Where did Jason learn to play chess? (*At the library*)
2. Why was Jason nervous? (*Any of these is correct: the other kids were older than he was; he did not know how to play; he thought the other kids would make fun of him*)
3. Did Jason learn to play chess? (*Yes*)
4. What do you think will happen tomorrow? (*Any reasonable answer is acceptable: he won; he lost; he had fun*)

CHILD PAGE: PASSAGE 301

Playing Chess

Last year Jason's mother took him to the library where children were playing chess in an after-school club. Jason thought it looked like fun. He decided he wanted to join the chess program. At first he was very afraid because most of the kids were older. He was afraid the other boys would laugh at him because he did not know how to play. But they were really nice to him and showed him how to play. Jason soon became an expert at chess. Tomorrow is Jason's big day: He is entering his first chess tournament! Good luck, Jason!

PARENT PAGE: GRADE 3 PASSAGE 302

Introduce this passage by telling your child it is about a birthday party. *(Children should be able to read this passage with no more than 2-3 errors.)*

Beth's Birthday Party

It was Beth's ninth birthday. She was going to have a party at the bowling alley near her house. Five of her friends were invited. Sadly, Beth got the flu and they could not have the party. Three weeks later, her mom surprised her with a pizza party. All her friends were there. They ate pizza on the picnic table in her back yard and then watched a DVD. They watched her favorite movie, *Alvin and the Chipmunks*. After the movie, they ate chocolate cake and chocolate ice cream. Everyone had a good time.

Read the following questions to your child after he finishes reading the story.

1. How old was Beth? (*9*)

2. What happened to Beth's party at the bowling alley? (*She got the flu, and it was cancelled*)

3. How did her mom surprise her? (*With a pizza party and movie at home or another party*)

4. What did they eat at the party? (*Any of these is acceptable: pizza, cake, and ice cream*)

5. What do you think is Beth's favorite flavor of ice cream? (*Chocolate*)

CHILD PAGE: PASSAGE 302

Beth's Birthday Party

It was Beth's ninth birthday. She was going to have a party at the bowling alley near her house. Five of her friends were invited. Sadly, Beth got the flu and they could not have the party. Three weeks later, her mom surprised her with a pizza party. All her friends were there. They ate pizza on the picnic table in her back yard and then watched a DVD. They watched her favorite movie, *Alvin and the Chipmunks*. After the movie, they ate chocolate cake and chocolate ice cream. Everyone had a good time.

APPENDIX E

Informal Screening for Children In Grades 4–12

Copyright 2015 Lorna Kaufman

The informal screening tests were developed to help parents determine whether or not their child needs help with reading and whether or not they should seek a professional, independent evaluation. These screening tests should not take the place of a professional evaluation. The **sole** purpose of the screening documents is to help parents decide whether or not they need to take the next step and have their child evaluated by a qualified professional.

By using the screening documents the reader acknowledges that he or she will only use them for the purpose described above—as a tool in their decision-making process to help decide whether or not to consult a professional independent evaluator with regard to their child's reading ability.

The screening documents should **never** be used for the following:

- ▶ To monitor a student's reading progress
- ▶ To determine a student's reading skills
- ▶ For purposes of an IEP
- ▶ For purposes of diagnosis

These documents are intended only for the use of the individual reader and duplication or distribution is prohibited.

INFORMAL SCREENING FOR CHILDREN IN GRADES 4–12

TESTING GUIDELINES

▶ Choose a time when your child is not tired or distracted. Keep in mind that children are often tired after school.

▶ Choose a quiet, well-lit room where you will not be interrupted.

▶ Sit at a table adjacent to your child (see video).

▶ If your child asks you for help with a word, first ask if he can sound it out. If he cannot, you can either tell him the word or just move on. This counts as an error.

▶ If your child gets stuck on a word, ask him if he can read the word. If not, say, "Let's move on." This counts as an error.

▶ Don't correct your child if he makes an error.

▶ Be encouraging to your child, no matter how much difficulty he has reading.

▶ Have your child leave the room before you score the test.

▶ If you find that your child has difficulty with the tests, *stop the testing*. Please do not become impatient with your child. Remember, he is doing the best he can. You have taken the first step, and now it is time for you to take the next one.

TEST PROCEDURE FOR STUDENTS IN GRADES 4–12

By the time students reach the fourth grade there is no longer specific reading instruction in the classroom that is aimed at teaching decoding skills. What you really need to know is whether your child can read and understand the grade-level material that is used in the classroom.

The procedure for an informal screening is quite simple for children in the fourth grade and above. Have your child bring home the science or social studies textbook that he is using in class. I recommend using the text from one of these two subjects because it is most informative to observe how your child is able to read passages of nonfiction—and how he is able to understand nonfiction material. If the teacher does not use a textbook, use one of the handouts that she gives the class.

- Make a copy of two pages of the book so you can follow along. The copy is for your use, and your child can read from the textbook.

- Select from a unit that the class finished studying about a month ago. I don't suggest selecting from the unit they are currently studying or from a unit that they have not yet covered.

- Ask him to read one or two pages *orally* to you.

- If he asks for help with a word, first ask him if he can sound it out; if he cannot, tell him the word. This counts as an error if you tell him the word.

- Mark a line through each word read incorrectly. Even if the student reads part of the word correctly, mark a line through it if there is any part omitted or mispronounced. For example, if the word is "walking" and the child reads "walk," mark a line through the word: ~~walk.~~

- Circle each word that the child *leaves out*. (This is an error.)

- Place a caret (∧) where extra words are *inserted*. (This is an error.)

- Excessive self-corrections and repetitions, while not scored here, can be indicative of problems with decoding. Do not worry about marking self-corrections and repeated words and phrases now, but be aware of their significance.

- Ask your child five or six questions about the passage. This will require you to pre-read the passage to identify the questions you want to ask.

- It is good to begin with a general question, such as, "Can you tell me about what you just read?"

- Try to determine whether your child has really grasped the "big picture" and a few details from the reading.

Can your child read the passage accurately and fluently, or does he struggle with many words and read slowly and laboriously? Can he answer comprehension questions about the material he has read?

If the answers to these questions are "no," it is time for you to seek an independent evaluation by a professional.

INDEX

academic ability, diagnostic evaluation of, *53–4*

accommodations, educational, *36–7, 44, 64, 71, 132, 137–9, 152–4, 195*

African-American children, reading problems and, *xx, 98*

age-equivalent (AE) scores, *77, 195*

alphabetics, *115*

American Indian children, reading problems and, *xx, 98*

anecdotal evidence, insufficiency of, *111*

assessments, informal, *13–14*

attention-deficit/hyperactivity disorder (ADHD), *2, 95, 101, 195, 198*

attorneys, special education, *160, 190, 201*

average scores. *See* mean (average) scores.

auditory processing disorders, *22–3, 41, 97, 195*

"balanced approach," *127*

behavioral indicators of reading problems, *17–19*

bell curve. *See* normal distribution of scores.

benchmarks, progress monitoring tests and, *6*

brain
neurological disorders, *22, 95, 195, 198*
reading and, *91–3*

Broad Reading scores, *82*

certification, teacher, *135–6, 141*

Chall, Jeanne, *112*

charter schools, special education services and, *159–60*

child-related risk factors, reading-problem, *99–101*

classroom observations, *48–50, 52, 61–2, 140–1*

cluster scores. *See* composite scores.

cognitive functioning, *42, 52–3, 196.* *See also* intelligence level, reading ability and.

Common Core state standards, *31, 124, 196*

composite scores, *81–3, 196*

consonant blends, *118, 196*

context, reading in, *57*

continuity of instruction, *44*

continuum of learning, reading ability and, xviii, *93–4*

criterion-referenced tests, *71–2, 85–6, 196*

cumulative process, learning to read as, *117, 120*

current level of performance, *152*

deafness, *100*

decoding ability

defined, *56, 196*

diagnostic evaluation of, *56–64*

fluency and, *122–3*

learning disabilities and, *96–7*

reading ability and, *91, 96–7, 123–5*

developmental indicators or reading problems, *19–23*

diagnostic evaluations

administration of, *47–50*

final report based upon, *64–5*

for K–3rd grades, *62–3*

for 4th–12th grades, *63–4*

school systems and, *39–45, 155–7, 167*

importance of, *35–9, 186*

insurance coverage of, *50*

scope of, *50–62*

source of behavioral issues and, *17*

unbiased and accurate, *45–6*

diagnosticians, quality, *47–50*

disruptive behaviors, reading problems and, *xvi, 17*

dyscalculia, *97, 197*

dysgraphia, *97, 197*

dyslexia, *92, 96–8, 194, 197, 200–1*

ear infections, chronic, *21–2, 100*

early grades, reading problems and, *12, 39, 94, 98, 103–5, 187. See also* early intervention.

early intervention

classroom teachers and, *6–8*

importance of, *1–5, 9–13, 184–5*

parents and, *5–6, 8–10, 185*

school systems and, *6–8, 185–5*

strategies for, *13–14*

See also early grades, reading problems and.

educational indicators of reading problems, *23–4*

educational risk factors, reading-problem, *99, 103–5*

Elementary and Secondary Education Act (No Child Left Behind), *147*

embedded phonics, *119, 127. See also* phonics.

encoding ability, diagnostic evaluation of, *60*

evaluations, special education, *148–50, 155–7*

evidence-based reading instruction, *12, 43–4, 110–1, 126, 129–33, 135, 147, 158, 178–9*

environmental risk factors, reading-problem, *99, 101–3*

executive functioning, *48–9, 197*

explicit instruction, *94, 119–20, 123–4, 187. See also* explicit, systematic phonics instruction.

explicit, systematic phonics instruction, *98, 104, 109, 117–20, 127, 129, 187, 202*

specific learning disabilities
and, *130, 149, 158, 201*
letters, proficiency with, *23*
limited English proficiency, *98, 102*
listening comprehension, vs. reading comprehension, *59*
low-performing schools, *99, 103–4*

mastery, teaching to, *114, 120–2*
mean (average) scores, *73–5, 78–9, 81, 83, 198*
measurable annual goals, *152*
measuring progress, standardized tests and, *84–6*
magnetoencephalography (MEG), *92*
memorization, rote, *24*
modifications, educational, *37, 64, 199*
multisensory structured language reading approaches, *117, 134–5, 140–1. See also* systematic and explicit phonics instruction.

National Institute of Child Health and Human Development (NICHD), *110–11*
National Reading Panel (NRP), *111*
neocortex, *91–2*
networking, *178*
neurological disorders, *22, 95, 195, 198. See also* brain, reading and.
No Child Left Behind (NCLB), *147, 199*
nonsense words, diagnostic evaluations and, *57*
nonstandard English, in home, *98, 102*

nonverbal learning disabilities (NVLDs), *97, 199*
nonverbal reasoning, *199*
normal distribution of scores, *78-80, 199*

occipital cortex, *91–2*
occupational therapists, *42*
oral language skills
developmentally delayed and, *19–20*
evaluation of, *52*
reading and, *20, 23, 90*
organizing ideas, difficulty with, *20–1*
orthographic processing, *199. See also* spelling ability.
Orton-Gillingham approach, *134*
Orton, Samuel Torrey, *134*
outcome tests, *70–1*
"outgrowing" reading problems, *4, 7, 10, 13*

parent advisory committees (PACs), *180, 199*
parents
as advocates, *163–6, 176–80, 183–94*
early intervention and, *5–6, 8–10*
instincts of, *5–6*
percentile rank, *75–81, 84–5, 140, 152, 200*
personal histories, in diagnostic evaluations, *52*
phonemes, *187, 200*
phonemic awareness, *200*
phonics
defined, *90, 200*

"embedded phonics" and, *119, 127*

explicit, systematic phonics instruction and, *98, 104, 109, 117–20, 127, 129, 187, 202*

phonics-based reading programs and, *57, 94, 98, 104, 109–14, 116–23, 126, 129, 134*

phonological awareness vs., *55*

skill with, *90–1, 93, 121*

teaching fluency and, *123*

whole language vs. *109–10, 127, 188*

phonological awareness, *54–5, 90, 111-12, 114-17, 129, 133, 187, 200*

physical therapists, *42*

poverty, literacy and, xviii, *99, 102–3*

private schools, special education services and, *159–60*

procedural safeguards, *60*

processing speed, *52, 200*

progress monitoring, *13, 57, 69–71, 84–5, 113, 122, 139–40, 158, 200*

progress monitoring tests and, *69–70*

psychologists, school, *42*

rapid naming, diagnostic evaluation of, *55*

raw scores, *72–3, 77, 200*

reading circuit, *91. See also* brain, reading and.

reading comprehension

decoding and, *56*

defined, *124, 200*

diagnostic evaluation of, *58–9*

instruction in, *30, 114, 123–5*

reading curriculum, evidenced-based, school-wide, *105–6, 126–7*

reading disabilities, *96–7, 101, 138, 149, 197, 200. See also* dyslexia

reading groups, *23, 121–2, 138–9*

reading instruction

"balanced approach" to, *127*

beginning readers and, *113–27*

determining school's approach to, *113, 187*

effective, *44–5, 114–25, 187–8*

evidence-based, *12, 43–4, 110–12, 126, 129–33, 135, 147, 158, 178–9*

lack of integrated, *105–6*

multisensory structured language reading approaches, *117, 134–5, 140–1*

phonics-based approach to, *57, 94, 98, 104, 109-14, 116–20, 127, 134, 188*

sight word approach to, *109, 187–8. See also* whole language.

whole-language-based approach to, *108–10, 112, 119–20, 127, 178, 202*

reading level, determining, *25–31*

by grade level, *26–31*

reading research, evidence-based, *110–12*

reading specialists, *105, 128–9, 135, 145*

reading to children, daily, *103*

"red flags," reading-problem, *16–24*

referrals, for special education services, *147–8*

religious schools, special education services and, *159–60*